To my parents,
Faride and Sayed.
For their love, inspiration
and endless support.

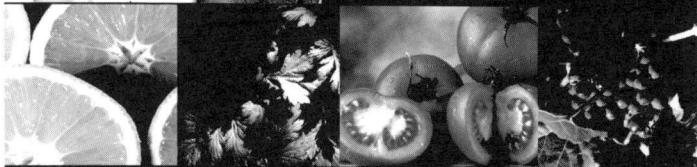

Dr. Pete's
Eating For A Healthy Heart

Exclusive Recipes Inside!

Includes a Guide to Living the Heart Healthy Way!

Pierre S. Aoukar, M.D.

With a forward by Dr. H. Karamanoukian, Cardiovascular Surgeon

Published in New York, 2003.

More Information at:
www.DiagnosisHeart.com

*"Let food be your medicine
and medicine your food."*

-Hippocrates

Acknowledgments

My sincerest gratitude to all those who helped in the publication of this book: first and foremost to Dr. K for being an extraordinary mentor, colleague and benefactor; to Freeman without whom this book would not be possible, you are a true friend and colleague; to Karen K for always making things happen; to Jo for her phenomenal design and graphics work; to my family, mom, dad, Maria, Elie, Patty, Jacque and Anthony, for bearing the brunt of my endless culinary experiments; to Marika and the Smith family for their love and encouragement; to Dr. Campbell for having the courage to do what is right, especially in the face of adversity and for inspiring me to do the same; to all those physicians and patients who have been my teachers; to my late grandmother, who looks on from the other side, thank you for guiding my hand through the work you first inspired; and to God, whose love motivates my daily effort.

Contents

More Information at:
www.CardiacNutrition.com

Foreword

Anyone who has ever struggled with coronary heart disease knows the importance of perspective. After all, it's not easy to have a great genetic make-up with relatives that lived to the ripe age of 100! For most of us, including close family members, there have been and will continue to be cardiovascular events in our lives. Some of these events will forever scar the heart and some will even cause premature death. In order to stay on track and minimize the ravages of coronary heart disease, it's helpful to fight the daily "battle of the bulge" by modifying the foods we eat in order to maximize our nutrient intake and harness the antioxidant effects of these foods. This, in combination with a healthy outlook on life, mental well-being, exercise and an appropriate check on daily stressors, will optimize the genetic milieu which is responsible for our "expected life span." After all, it is not yet possible to modify our genetic constitution to reduce the risks of acquiring coronary heart disease. Therefore, we can only make inroads into cardiovascular fitness by eating right and taking care of our bodies.

Collectively, optimal nutrition is extremely important to all of us. As a physician and heart surgeon, I know that if one lives long enough, one will acquire heart disease. As a matter of fact, the Bogalusa Heart Study demonstrated the early ravages of atherosclerosis in children as young as 6 years of age! This is what obsesses the Type A personalities amongst us. If we know that these things occur, how can we "take control" of our bodies and change the course of acquired heart disease? Is it possible to modify our physical environment so that we can prevent coronary heart disease? The answer is an absolute YES! Dr. Pete comes from a family with significant history of coronary heart disease. He was motivated to go to medical school because his father had heart surgery at the age of 35. This personal experience, combined with unique educational opportunities, has led him to institute lifestyle modifications resulting in an astounding cholesterol profile. At this rate, his life expectancy exceeds 80 years and, even with his family history, his chances of developing coronary heart disease are minuscule.

Most of us are not obsessed with what appropriate "cardiac nutrition" is; we inappropriately channel our energies to lose weight. This interferes with our sense of well-being and can hinder our enjoyment of life. The essence of what we are is what we eat! Dr. Pete has forever changed my focus on what I eat. I have in turn passed on his recipes to my patients and their families. I have changed my eating habits in a permanent way, using a holistic approach. Eating good foods starts with an active process of preparing good foods. Once the goal is redirected to "eating healthy" and not to "losing weight," a holistic effort is made to treat the whole body and the whole person.

Dr. Pete has written an excellent book that points us to a holistic approach towards eating well and staying healthy. The focus is not calories but eating the right things. This optimizes cholesterol profiles and tightens blood sugar levels, improves blood pressure and perhaps reduces the stresses of daily life. I recommend reading his book and considering his "edible" philosophies for healthy living. You will forever change your life and, perhaps, prolong it to its maximal extent!

HL Karamanoukian, MD
Heart Surgeon
Buffalo General Hospital
Assistant Professor of Surgery
University at Buffalo

Introduction

The majority of people you know will die of heart disease. There is not a person in this country who has not been affected by this plague. The fight against heart disease wages on and it is, in the least, a multi-faceted battle. Treatments used by medicine and surgery leave many other options with which you can reduce your risk of heart disease. These are known as lifestyle modifications, the most important of which are diet, exercise and stress. As you can surmise from the title of this book, the focus here will be the food you eat. This is not to say, however, that diet is the most influential of the three. On the contrary, reducing your risk of heart disease through lifestyle requires a synergistic balance of healthy diet, regular exercise and stress reduction. The key to successful prevention is maximizing each in your daily life. My goal in putting this guide together was to aid you in developing a regular diet of foods you will enjoy eating while at the same time boosting your cardiac health.

Later, I will tell you the personal story of how I came to do the work I now do and what it was that motivated me to focus part of that work on a cardiac maintenance diet. Before I go any further, however, you must understand that this book is not a fad diet. It is not about a temporary regimen that will totally change your life in a few months. Don't get me wrong. This book could and will help you completely change your life if you wish to do so. Know that eating heart healthy is a permanent change in the way you live and eat. It requires dedication and patience and it assumes flexibility and a willingness to try new things. Whether you have heart disease, a family history of heart disease or no association with heart disease at all, you will stand to benefit from eating a heart healthy diet.

At the beginning, results will come quickly because your body will be adjusting to major changes. This is the most difficult part of your lifestyle modification and requires your greatest effort. As you become accustomed to eating these foods, your body will reach a new equilibrium. When you reach this equilibrium, your decisions about eating will become effortless and these decisions will begin to positively influence other factors of life affecting your cardiac health. There is a rather old term to describe that which has come into new practice, holistic medicine—medicines which treat the whole body, the whole person. In this case, the medicine is food. What foods am I talking about, specifically?

The basis for my recipes is a plant-based or vegan diet—a vegetarian diet which contains no animal products, such as meat, poultry, fish, eggs or dairy—which is, with few exceptions, also a diet low in fat. Medical research has repeatedly shown the benefits of eating a diet high in plant foods, not only for the prevention of heart disease, but for preventing and treating other chronic diseases, such as cancer, stroke and diabetes. Modern pioneers of this type of diet include Dr. T. Colin Campbell of the Cornell-Oxford-China Project, Dr. Dean Ornish and Dr. John McDougall, names which may seem familiar. What I have attempted to do is create recipes which are not only good for your heart, but are a joy to eat and prepare. Furthermore, you are encouraged to experiment with the recipes, use them as you wish and at your own comfort level. This book is meant as a guide rather than a plan. I do not expect most or any of you to become strict vegetarians after using the book. What I hope you will do is find a way to incorporate heart healthy foods into your daily life to the extent that you will enjoy eating them. You deserve the best quality of life. Medicine can merely present you the option of obtaining that quality. I am offering you your most favorable chances of achieving that life.

To Your Health,
Pierre S. Aoukar, MD

The Environment and Your Heart

Eighteen years ago, my father underwent open heart surgery for double coronary bypass grafting. He was 35 years old. He was so young and in such good shape that doctors did not even consider heart disease when he first presented with chest pain. In fact, his doctor sent him home three times with the diagnosis of acid reflux. I believe he quickly changed doctors after that. My father's case is the exception; but nonetheless, you don't know whom heart disease will strike or when. There is no doubt that in the future, with the help of genetics, we will be able to predict who is likely to develop certain diseases. However, a future diagnosis does not mean a future cure. We are far from being able to manipulate our DNA into the perfect double-helix. The key to successful treatment of heart disease lies in prevention. In order to understand this, let us take a look at the interaction between genetics, lifestyle and our environment.

Genetics is undoubtedly the cutting edge and a final frontier of medicine. We have made great strides in mapping out the entire human genome, but we don't yet have the knowledge to make use of it. In the future, we'll be able to look at a single cell from the body, determine which DNA elements are damaged or imperfect and perhaps, far into the future be able to fix the DNA itself. Prior to having that ability, we shall be able to look at your DNA, determine which diseases you are at risk to develop and attempt to eliminate that risk with the tools of modern medicine. However, we are also still far from this stage in the genetics of disease. What we do know is that to a certain extent—and the magnitude is different for every person—your genes, or DNA, predispose you to developing diseases. What we also know is that environmental factors, such as diet, exercise, smoking and stress, affect the expression of that DNA. In other words, the way you live your life helps determine which diseases you develop based on your DNA. Your DNA can make you more susceptible to lung cancer for example, if you smoke. Or your DNA can make your artery walls more likely to have plaques if you eat a high fat diet. This is the way in which, for the majority of us, genetics affect disease. For an unfortunate few, genes are the direct cause of their disease and regardless of what environmental risk factors a person controls, the outcome will be the same. But, remember, this is the exception rather than the rule. For most of us, our genes will play an indirect role in the evolution of disease. You can think of your genes as the middlemen that control your interaction between the environment and the progression of disease in your body. Therefore, until we are able to manipulate genes, the best we can do is control our environment—that means lifestyle.

Lifestyle—what you eat, how active you are, your level of stress, smoking, drinking, your contentment with life—constitutes the majority of your environment and the environmental risks to your body. So far, there is little we can do to control genes themselves, but our environment is a whole different ball game. For the moment, put aside toxic waste, pesticides and radiation exposure. Except for specific instances, these play such a minor role in disease processes that for our purposes, they are not worth worrying about. What you need to worry about are the things you do on a daily basis— the things from this world which have the most intimate contact with your body. For continuity, let's take food as an example. Most of us eat between three and five times a day. Food comes in contact with about 27 feet of intestine and a surface area of about 4000 square feet or the equivalent of two tennis courts. Throughout digestion there is only a single layer of cells standing as a barrier between the inside of your body and the outside world—that is, the food you've just eaten. The interaction at this microscopic level is so complex and intimate, we have only begun to understand the specific details of what happens. If this is beginning to worry you, it should. Diet is a powerful environmental risk factor.

Cigarette smoke, as another example, is full of carcinogens and carbon monoxide, which are, in reality, poisons; yet smokers (and non-smokers) repeatedly expose their lungs—with a surface area the size of one tennis court—to this vile plume. Again, only one cell layer stands to defend your lungs against the toxins contained in tobacco smoke. Smoking is not only the leading cause of lung cancer, but the most preventable cause of death overall. According to the Harvard School of Public Health, by the year 2020, tobacco is expected to kill more people than any single disease, surpassing even the HIV epidemic.[1] When it comes to smoking, there is only one option: don't smoke and if you do, take any means possible to quit. Before you even begin to contemplate any other changes in your life, this must be the first.

---

[1] *http://www.hshp.harvard.edu/organizations/bdu/summary.html*

We are a sedentary nation. Does it take much to walk up one or two flights of stairs? Yet, I continually see people riding the elevator up or down one flight. In order for exercise to have an effect, you must do it regularly. One of the best ways is to incorporate it into all aspects of your daily life. Make a conscious effort to take the stairs, park in the far lot so you have to walk to your car, and take a walk during lunch. Certainly, this alone is not enough for daily exercise, but it adds up. I recommend doing one hour of exercise, at least five times a week for everyone healthy enough to do it. You don't have to run, swim or cycle, though these are certainly good for you. Walking is one of my favorite exercises and it's one of the best for you. Any activity which gives your heart a workout counts. By the way, those stairs also count towards your one hour a day. In addition to conditioning your heart to pump more efficiently and trimming inches off your waistline, exercise releases natural chemicals from your brain called endorphins. Endorphins help elevate your mood and give you natural highs. They are just one more testament to the effect lifestyle has on your health. As a side note, always check with your physician before beginning any exercise program.

So, besides taking your medications, you should quit smoking, eat right and exercise regularly. That's asking a lot, but it still is not enough. Did you know that it takes twice as many muscles to frown as it does to smile? Do you remember the last time you were not stressed out about something? Save your energy for the walks. Stress, like high blood pressure, is a silent killer. It exists and sometimes you acknowledge it, but it is difficult to recognize the effect it has on your body. Stress is a difficult topic, because so many things that stress us are outside of our control. What we can control is our reaction to these stressors. Relaxation techniques like yoga and tai chi are definitely beneficial, but so is making time for activities you enjoy—activities which will not only take your mind off those stressors, but also elevate your mood and give you clarity to better deal with problems. Don't forget that exercise can help significantly because of those wonderful endorphins which will naturally put you in a happier state of mind.

There were a few things I neglected to mention about my father. Although he was 35 when he first presented with symptoms of heart disease, in many ways he also had set the stage for eventual problems. Before his operation, he smoked 2 packs per day for 18 years, he had a very stressful job with no time to relax because of four young kids and he ate a diet high in fat and meat. When you take the time to examine the environment in which you live, you recognize the many things that need improvement. My father changed his life drastically since his first surgery. He quit smoking immediately, began to exercise regularly and followed a strict vegetarian diet. I was in fourth the grade when all this happened, but I remember it as if it were now. I am happy to say that my father is in good health and is still leading the heart healthy life he began 18 years ago.

I did not realize the full extent to which my father's experience would influence me until my junior year in college. I had already been a vegetarian for two years because I never really enjoyed eating meat and at the time I believed it was also an expression of liberation on my part. Nonetheless, I had been working as a student chef for those two years at the Statler Hotel, the teaching hotel of Cornell University, an establishment run completely by students. So my interest and skills in the culinary arts were blossoming. That year I had embarked on a quest to complete requirements for the nutrition major as well as for a degree in chemistry. A few days into the fall semester, I ran across a poster detailing a new course in vegetarian nutrition. As you can imagine, I could hardly contain my excitement. The course had little to do with vegetarian nutrition as I had known it. It would change my life forever.

Vegetarian nutrition was taught by Dr. T. Colin Campbell, lead author of the Cornell-Oxford-China Project. The focus was the effects of diet on the development of chronic diseases such as heart disease, cancer and stroke. Speakers included famous names like Dr. Esselstyn of the Cleveland Clinic, Dr. John McDougall and Dr. Dean Ornish. The common conclusion these scientists had come to was that a low fat, plant-based diet was optimal for preventing and treating chronic disease. Convinced that my family history had already placed me in a high risk group, I decided to try this experiment on myself. Keeping everything else the same—exercise, stress factors—I changed my diet to include only plant-based foods. In three months, I dropped my cholesterol from 220 to 130 mg/dl. I had incidentally lost weight without trying, my energy level was higher than ever and I was happy. Seven years later, I am still living the same way. My cholesterol remains the same, I have an incredible amount of energy and I could never go back to eating the foods which were destroying my body. Most importantly, I had optimized the environment in which I lived. Incidentally, my calling had found me.

Feeding Your Heart

The synergistic forces of my life had set forth a unique challenge: how to make heart healthy food that I and others will want to eat. My love of cooking and eating fine foods would not allow me to sacrifice taste and quality for health. The culmination of my efforts to conquer that challenge comprises this book.

To begin, you can seldom eat too many vegetables and fruits. They are made mostly of water, fiber and carbohydrates. With few exceptions, they are bulky, not calorie dense and contain nearly all the vitamins and minerals your body needs. In fact, humans survive and thrive on fruits and vegetables alone, but will quickly die on an all meat diet because of water-soluble vitamin deficiencies (the first being vitamin C). The only vitamin not found in plant foods is vitamin B12, though there is some controversy about bacteria in the human intestine synthesizing B12. Nonetheless, it is a wise idea to supplement a plant-based diet with oral B12 tablets (except for pernicious anemia which requires B12 injections). The neurological consequences of a deficiency of this vitamin are serious and irreversible.

Fruits, vegetables and whole grains provide the majority of fiber in any person's diet. The fiber, in turn, helps to excrete a portion of our body's cholesterol, effectively lowering blood lipid levels. These foods are also extremely rich in antioxidants; powerful agents which help protect your artery walls from damage. In other words, fruits and vegetables are most beneficial to your health, but you knew that because your mother told you so.

What can make healthy foods unhealthy is the type and amount of fat added to foods, which is why it is always preferable to cook your own food. You control the fat content because you control what goes in. Of all your environmental risk factors, dietary fat is most influential in affecting blood cholesterol levels. Too much total fat or too much saturated fat (found in meats, eggs and dairy foods) will raise LDL or bad cholesterol. Olive oil can help to raise HDL or good cholesterol. Exercise has a more pronounced effect on boosting HDL. In my home, I have only one type of oil, extra-virgin olive oil. All the recipes in this book, when necessary, use only olive oil and a few use tahini (sesame seed paste). No other type of fat has as beneficial an effect on the heart as extra-virgin olive oil. This is due to the high proportion of monounsaturated fat and the amount of antioxidants. In my opinion, no other type of fat or oil tastes better. I will leave that for you to decide. Buy a good bottle of extra-virgin olive oil (it's worth the money) and see the difference it makes in the flavor of your food. You will never go back to using anything else.

The amount of fat is equally important as the type. According to the US dietary guidelines, you can consume up to 30% of your daily calories from fat. Unless you are an infant or toddler, you certainly do not need more than 15% of your total daily calories from fat and 20% at most. This translates into 30 to 40 grams of fat per day. 0% of your daily calories should come from saturated fat. It is fine to have a little saturated fat, once in a while, but remember saturated fat has the most negative effect on your heart (only one of my recipes—"Cream Cheese" Frosting—contains a significant amount of saturated fat). Cholesterol is produced only by animals and it is only foods of animal origin which contain cholesterol. Therefore, a purely plant-based diet never contains cholesterol. It's that simple.

You will notice that nutrition labels are missing from all the recipes. This was purposely done because I do not believe in counting—counting calories, counting fat grams, counting fiber. I did this for a few years and found that it made eating laborious and unenjoyable. This is not to say you should stop reading nutrition labels. By all means, it is necessary that you read food labels. After a while you will get to know the fat and calorie content of foods without even looking. What you should not do is meticulously keep track of the calories and fat you consume at every meal. It is advisable to have a rough estimate of the amount of fat you've eaten in a day. However, if you eat properly, you will find that this takes care of itself. I almost never purchase prepared food that has more than 5 grams of fat per serving and most of the time; the amount is less than 3 grams. This is an easy way to control the amount of fat in prepared foods. In foods you cook, it is equally simple. One cardinal piece of advice: do not eat fried foods. Foods that are fried have an incredibly high content of fat that doesn't necessarily enhance the flavor or texture of foods. In my recipes, you will learn ways to cook delicious foods without frying. Olive oil and, in fact, all oils contain 14 grams of fat per tablespoon. If you use two tablespoons per serving, you know you should cut back on your fat intake for the remainder of the day. It's that easy. Except for nuts, seeds, olives, avocados and coconuts, I can think of few other foods with a significant amount fat; so unless you consume large portions of these foods on a regular basis, you should never have to worry about the fat content of fruits and vegetables you eat. I do recommend incorporating nuts into your regular diet, in small amounts. One nut in particular stands out above the rest: almonds. For the amount of fat they contain, almonds are higher in protein (except for peanuts) and vitamin content (including calcium) than any other nut.

On another note, if you consume too many of your calories at once, regardless of where those excess calories come from, they will be stored as fat. In addition, bigger meals result in sustained high blood sugar. Therefore, five meals a day is preferable to two or three. Eat three larger meals at breakfast, lunch and dinner, with two snacks in between. This is optimal for maintaining tight blood sugar levels and upping your body's metabolism. As for total amount of calories, you need not count. Eat until you are satiated and never more. You will find it difficult to gain weight by eating smaller meals more frequently. Gaining weight on a diet where the majority of calories come from carbohydrates is a valid concern. If you are worried about overeating, or gaining weight, here are a few helpful hints. Do not eat later in the evening. Try to eat your last meal before 7 p.m . (or at least 3 hours before you go to sleep). This lessens the chance that the food you've eaten will be stored as fat. Furthermore, if you find that you are still hungry after eating a full meal, drink a large glass water (this fills you and also aids in digestion) and wait fifteen or twenty minutes. If you are still hungry, listen to your body and eat.

The majority of your carbohydrates, except for the occasional dessert and daily fruits, should be complex carbohydrates—this means whole grain breads, pasta, high fiber cereals and rice. Whenever you can, opt for whole grain foods. They are higher in nutrients and fiber than their processed counterparts and lower in simple sugars. Although getting enough protein is always a concern with vegetarian diets, this concern is neither valid nor warranted. As long as you eat a variety of grains, vegetables and legumes (including soy products), you will not have difficulty obtaining enough protein, even if you are physically very active.

You have probably heard that salt can cause high blood pressure. In susceptible people, salt can help elevate blood pressure by retaining water, but salt is never the direct cause of high blood pressure. Furthermore, in 90% of people with high blood pressure, we do not know the cause. In fact, salt should be a part of everyone's diet because it is essential for life (blood is basically salt water with different proteins mixed in). It is a necessary seasoning which makes food palatable and for many constitutes a major source of iodine, a mineral essential to metabolism. The danger is in overusing salt. Use the minimum amount you need to make foods taste good and avoid processed foods high in sodium (avoid processed foods all together if you can). Talk to your physician to see how sodium fits into your diet.

You have probably also heard that a couple of alcoholic drinks a day can do you some good. The latest research does show that two drinks per day for males and one drink per day for females has some cardiovascular benefit. Consuming above the recommended amount, however, negates these benefits and is actually harmful. I would personally suggest red wine because of the added benefits from antioxidants.

Along the same lines, fish consumption has also been said to confer cardiovascular benefit, mainly due to the antioxidant effects of omega-3 fatty acids found primarily in cold water fish (salmon, trout, tuna, snapper). I personally do not eat fish, but if you enjoy it, fish certainly can be part of a heart healthy diet. If you do not like fish, flax seed is a wonderful plant source of omega-3 fatty acids and it contains more omega-3s per serving than any variety of cold water fish.

Getting started is difficult, especially if this will be a dramatic change for you. Take your time and go slowly. For changes to be effective it is best they occur over an extended period of time. The optimal time, in fact, is 12 weeks. For some, this will be a tremendous challenge, so be patient. In times when I was overburdened with the challenges of life, my father would always tell me, if life were simple and there were no challenges or problems to solve, life would be boring. If you want excitement in your life, you need challenges. Get excited about this wonderful challenge, about trying new foods that will tantalize your palette and simultaneously rejuvenate your body and heart. Above all, enjoy the food you eat. Do not concern yourself with losing weight. With time and the right decisions that will happen. The true state of health you can not see on the outside; you feel it on the inside. You will experience through these recipes how delicious healthy food truly can be.

RECIPES

Appetizers and Side Dishes

Hot Ajvar

Servings: 6

INGREDIENTS:

2 large eggplants
4 sweet red peppers
juice of 1-2 large fresh lemons
2 medium cloves fresh garlic, finely crushed
¾ tsp. sea salt to taste
2 Tbs. extra-virgin olive oil
fresh flat leaf parsley, chopped

optional: fresh red hot chilies or crushed red pepper

DIRECTIONS:

1. Over an open flame (I use my stovetop), roast eggplants on all sides until completely wilted and charred. The smoke and aroma will fill your house, so make sure your kitchen is well ventilated, or grill the eggplant (whole) outside. Place the eggplants in a paper bag until cool. This will make them easier to clean. Once they are cooled, discard the stem and all the skin. If the seeds are large and overly abundant, discard them, since they will be bitter (if this is the case you will want to use one more eggplant). Otherwise use the whole eggplant. Do the same with the red peppers.

2. Using a wooden pestle or potato masher or fork, mash the eggplant and red peppers together like you would a potato until you have a uniform mixture. Do not use a food processor or blender (this will create a runny Ajvar). Add the remainder of the ingredients and stir until they are all blended. Adjust the lemon juice according to your taste. Garnish with parsley.

3. The origins of this dish are from eastern Europe. It is traditionally eaten as a spicy spread on bread, the same way hummus is eaten. To make this dish a little spicy you can prepare some red hot chilies the same way as the eggplant and sweet peppers and add them into the recipe or you can just add crushed red pepper.

Baba Ganoush

Servings: 4

INGREDIENTS:

2 large eggplants
1/4 cup Tahini
juice of 2-3 large fresh lemons
2 medium cloves fresh garlic, finely crushed
¾ tsp. sea salt

Optional: extra-virgin olive oil

DIRECTIONS:

1. Over an open flame (I use my stovetop), roast eggplant on all sides until completely wilted and charred. The smoke and aroma will fill your house, so make sure your kitchen is well ventilated, or grill the eggplant (whole) outside. Place the eggplants in a paper bag until cool. This will make them easier to clean. Once they are cooled, discard the stem and all the skin. If the seeds are large and overly abundant, discard them, since they will be bitter (if this is the case you will want to use one more eggplant). Otherwise use the whole eggplant.

2. Using a wooden pestle or potato masher or fork, mash the eggplant like you would a potato into fine stringy pieces. Do not use a food processor or blender (this will create a runny Baba). Add the remainder of the ingredients and stir until they are all blended. Adjust the lemon juice according to your taste. In addition, to cut down on the fat content you can make this dish with a bit of olive oil instead of tahini. Garnish either dish with extra-virgin olive oil.

Escarole Sauté

Servings: 2

INGREDIENTS:

1 ½-2 pounds or two heads escarole
8 cloves fresh garlic, thinly sliced
1 ½ Tbs. extra-virgin olive oil
sea salt to taste
crushed black pepper to taste
crushed red pepper, pinch
fresh lemon (optional)

DIRECTIONS:

1. Wash and dry the escarole as necessary. You can buy prepackaged escarole mixed greens. That will work for this recipe as well (use two packages). Chop the escarole into 2 inch pieces.

2. In a large nonstick skillet over low heat, add the oil and garlic. Brown the garlic lightly. Turn heat to medium. Add the escarole in batches. It will begin to wilt immediately. Intermittently toss with the garlic and oil. Cook until all the escarole is wilted. Turn heat off. Add salt and pepper as you wish. I like to squeeze a little fresh lemon juice on mine as well. This green makes an excellent side dish for pasta.

Falafel

Yields 3 dozen falafel balls

INGREDIENTS:

½ pound dried chickpeas (soaked overnight)
½ pound dried fava beans (soaked overnight)
8 cloves fresh garlic
6 green onions (scallions) or 1 large yellow onion
2 jalapenos, seeded
1 large bunch fresh Italian parsley, stems cut off
2 tsp. ground cumin
2 tsp. ground coriander
½ tsp. ground allspice
½ tsp. cayenne pepper
½ tsp. fresh ground black pepper
3 Tbs. hulled, untoasted sesame seeds
2 Tbs. sea salt
4-5 Tbs. white flour
1 Tbs. baking powder

Tahini Dressing*

DIRECTIONS:

1. Please do not substitute canned beans for dried beans. For one thing they are more expensive and for another they will not make good falafel. Make sure the beans are soaked overnight. Drain and combine half of each of the beans with all the garlic and onion into a large food processor. Process until all of the garlic is finely chopped. Add the remaining beans and process until the beans have a fine homogenous texture.

2. Add the remainder of the ingredients, except the sesame seeds, flour and baking powder. Process until all the ingredients are well blended and the parsley is finely chopped. Add the baking powder and some of the flour. The mixture will start to come together. The falafel mixture should hold together if you make a clump with your fist. Add the remainder of the flour as necessary. Finally, blend in the sesame seeds.

3. There are two ways to make a good falafel. First, you can deep-fry the falafel. This is what is traditionally done and is a treat once in a while, but it doesn't do your heart any good. (If you still want to fry, use peanut oil at 350°F. Shape the falafel into balls using a falafel maker, which you can buy cheaply at any Middle Eastern grocer. Fry the falafel on both sides until they are a golden brown). For a healthier version, which is what I like to do, you can pan fry the falafel. In a nonstick skillet over medium heat, use extra-virgin or regular olive oil to barely coat the pan. Fry the falafel on both sides until golden brown.

4. Once you make the mixture, falafel freeze well for about three months. They are best when cooked fresh, so never cook them ahead of time. To make a falafel sandwich use either pocket pita or large thin Lebanese pita. Flatten each falafel with your fingertips and use 3 to 4 falafel for each sandwich. Add tomatoes, fresh mint, pickled turnips, pickled wild cucumber, mixed greens, tahini dressing and, if you like, hot sauce.

*See Sauces and Dressings

Fresh Fava Beans

Servings: 4

INGREDIENTS:

2 pounds fresh tender fava beans
2 jalapenos, deseeded and deveined, julienned
8 cloves fresh garlic, coarsely crushed
2 Tbs. extra-virgin olive oil
sea salt to taste

fresh pita

DIRECTIONS:

This dish can only be made if the fava beans are very fresh and tender because you will be using the entire bean. Therefore this dish is usually only good in season, but it's very tasty. Fresh fava beans are also an acquired taste. Try them out and see for yourself. Wash the fava beans and snap each into large bite size pieces. In a large sauce pan, add oil, jalapenos and garlic. Sauté until garlic is lightly browned. Add the fava beans and salt. Cover and cook over medium heat, stirring occasionally. The beans are done when they are wilted, lightly browned and little or no liquid remains (20-30 minutes). Season for salt and pepper. Enjoy warm or cold, with fresh hot pita.

Hummus

Servings: 8-12

INGREDIENTS:

1 pound dried garbanzo beans (chick peas)
1/8 to ¼ cup Tahini
juice of 2 large fresh lemons
2 medium cloves fresh garlic
¾ tsp. sea salt

Optional: 1/8 cup extra-virgin olive oil

DIRECTIONS:

1. Cook the chick peas (garbanzo beans) according to package directions to doneness (either soak overnight and boil the next day, or for same day use: boil for 5 minutes, let sit one hour and boil to doneness). **SAVE** the water they were cooked in.

2. In a food processor mix ½ the chick peas, 2 cloves garlic and ¼ cup of boiled water from chickpeas. Blend to coarse texture. Add remainder of the chickpeas, lemon juice, salt and either ¼ cup tahini or 1/8 cup extra-virgin olive oil and 1/8 cup tahini. (Traditionally, the olive oil is drizzled on top, but for convenience -sandwiches and such- I have become accustomed to putting the olive oil into the hummus itself. This also cuts back on the total fat content of the dish.) Process until smooth. Add small amounts of the boiled water to adjust the thickness of the hummus.

VARIATIONS:

You can add many things to your hummus for variation. I like to add the following all at once:
1 Tbs. toasted cumin seed, 1 tsp. dried mint, 1 tsp. garam masala, 1 tsp. dried oregano, and either some crushed red pepper or a very thick hot sauce to taste.

In addition, Hummus is superb with fresh mint, pickles and fresh summer vegetables.

Portabella Steak

Servings: 4

INGREDIENTS:

8 large or 12 small portabella mushrooms, stems removed
8 cloves fresh minced garlic
1¼ cups balsamic vinegar
¼ cup extra-virgin olive oil
sea salt and black pepper to taste

DIRECTIONS:

1. Using a mini blender or a whisk, combine the vinegar, garlic, olive oil, salt and pepper. In a deep casserole dish, begin stacking the mushrooms stem side up. Fill each mushroom with the marinade and place the next mushroom on top of it until all the mushrooms and marinade are used up. Marinate for at least 2 hours and overnight if possible.

2. You can grill these on either an open or a double-sided grill. To grill, place the mushrooms stem side up over low to medium heat. Cover the grill if yours has a cover. Do NOT flip the mushrooms. If you do, you're going to lose all the good juices. Cook the mushrooms for 10 to 15 minutes without flipping. They are done when the edges start to wilt and flatten. It is always better to undercook than to overcook. You can use the leftover marinade to make a salad dressing.

3. Serve warm with a side of potatoes and your favorite salad. These steaks can be cooked ahead of time, refrigerated and used in a salad or sandwich or warmed up as a side dish.

Baked Tofu

INGREDIENTS:

2 pounds firm or extra-firm tofu, (not silken)
2-3 cups marinade, either Spicy Garlic Sauce* or Asian Dipping Sauce*

DIRECTIONS:

1. Slice each block of tofu into about 8 slices. Place the slices in a deep dish. For your marinade you can use either the spicy garlic sauce or the Asian dipping sauce. If you are going to use the garlic sauce, I would recommend adding water (equal to half the amount of sauce you will be using) to the sauce since it is fairly thick. Be sure to use enough marinade to cover all the tofu. Marinate for at least 2 hours or overnight.

2. When you are ready to bake, preheat the oven to 300°F.

3. Spray a sheet pan generously with nonstick cooking spray. Place the tofu in a single layer on the pan. Pour the entire marinade into the pan as well. Bake on a rack in the lower third of the oven until all the marinade has evaporated, the tofu is golden brown in color and firm in texture (it springs back to the touch). Approximate cooking time is one hour.

4. Cool at room temperature. Place in a tight plastic container until needed. This tofu is also great in stir-fries, Asian salads, sandwiches or just by itself.

* See Sauces and Dressings

Barbecue Tofu "Wingdings"

Servings: 2

INGREDIENTS:

1 pound firm or extra-firm tofu
1 recipe Nana Saul's Barbecue Sauce*
Non-stick cooking spray

DIRECTIONS:

1. Slice the block of tofu into ½ inch thick pieces. If you want you can marinate the tofu for an hour before cooking or even overnight. I find with this recipe that it is not necessary to marinate the tofu. (To marinate: drain the water in the container. Slice the tofu. In a deep dish or the container it came in, add enough marinade to cover the tofu completely.)

2. There are several ways to grill tofu. I've found best results using an open grill. Using a grill that cooks both sides at the same time yields variable results. Many times the tofu will lose its form completely from the weight of the top grill. Preheat your grill to medium. Spray the grill thoroughly with non-stick cooking spray and lay the slices of tofu onto the grill. Spray the side of tofu facing up with non-stick spray as well, so it does not stick when you flip it. When one side has browned well, flip tofu slices over. Brush barbecue sauce generously onto the side that has been cooked. When the other side is cooked, turn the slices over again and brush the other side with sauce. Cook for only two minutes. Remove from the grill and brush with additional sauce if desired.

* See Sauces and Dressings

Grilled Tofu

INGREDIENTS:

2 pounds firm or extra-firm tofu, (not silken)
2-3 cups marinade, either Spicy Garlic Sauce* or Asian Dipping Sauce*

DIRECTIONS:

1. For your marinade you can use either the spicy garlic sauce or the Asian dipping sauce. If you are going to use the garlic sauce, I would recommend adding water (equal to one-third the amount of sauce you will be using) to the sauce since it is fairly thick. Drain the water from the container. Leave the tofu as a whole block. In a deep dish or the container it came in, add enough marinade to cover the tofu completely. You want to marinade this tofu overnight.

2. There are several ways to grill tofu. I've found best results using an open grill. Using a grill that cooks both sides at the same time yields variable results. Many times the tofu will lose its form completely from the weight of the top grill. To grill, place the block over low heat. Cover the grill if yours has a cover. Cook on both sides until there is a uniform golden brown and charred texture to the outside. Cooking time is at least ½ hour.

3. Cool at room temperature. Place in a tight plastic container until needed. This tofu is great in stir-fries, Asian salads, sandwiches or just by itself.

* See Sauces and Dressings

Pan-fried Tofu

Servings: 2

INGREDIENTS:

1 pound firm or extra-firm tofu, (not silken)
2/3 cup Asian Dipping Sauce*
nonstick cooking spray

DIRECTIONS:

1. Slice the block of tofu into bite size pieces, about ½ inch thick. Spray a nonstick pan with cooking spray and place it over medium heat. Throw in the tofu and spray it with cooking spray so that when you flip the pieces they will not burn or stick. Cook on one side until light brown. Flip and cook on the other side until light brown.

2. Turn the heat up to high and add all the dipping sauce. Reduce the tofu in the cooking sauce until all the liquid has evaporated.

3. An alternative way to do this is to cook your sauce with the tofu. Once the tofu has cooked, add the garlic and ginger and sauté until browned. Add the remainder of the sauce ingredients, premixed. Reduce until all the liquid has evaporated.

4. The tofu is ready to enjoy as is, over rice, in a stir-fry, Asian salads or however you like.

* See Sauces and Dressings

Homemade Croutons

INGREDIENTS:

stale bread, any variety
fresh chopped garlic
extra-virgin olive oil
dried oregano
dried basil
dried or fresh parsley (optional)
cayenne pepper
paprika
sea salt to taste
crushed black pepper to taste

DIRECTIONS:

This recipe is great because you don't have to measure out anything. It's also fun to try this one with kids.

1. Preheat oven to 350°F.

2. You can do this recipe with fresh bread as well. The bread, however, will be easier to cut if it is allowed to sit uncovered at room temperature for at least a day. You want to cut the bread into bite-sized pieces, about ¾ inch cubes.

3. In a large bowl, pour extra-virgin olive oil to cover the bottom and add a handful of garlic. Add a quarter handful of oregano, basil, parsley, and paprika. Add a sprinkling of salt, cayenne pepper and black pepper. Throw in enough bread to just fill the bowl. Toss until all the bread pieces are well coated. Taste for salt and oil content. Add more as you feel necessary. The oil will expand when you cook the croutons, so you don't want to add too much. Besides, you don't want greasy croutons.

4. Spread the coated bread onto a sheet pan, so that each pieces touches the bottom of the pan. Cook in the middle or top racks of the oven until the croutons are a uniform golden brown and allow to cool on the sheet pan. Store in a tight-sealed plastic container until you need them. They make a tasty snack!

Garlic Bread

INGREDIENTS:

crusty Italian or French bread
extra-virgin olive oil
fresh crushed garlic
sea salt to taste
crushed red pepper
fresh or dried oregano
fresh marjoram

DIRECTIONS:

1. Preheat oven to 450°F.

2. This is one of those recipes where you can just wing it and it will always taste great. The most important ingredient, actually, is the bread. Make sure you buy the best quality bread you can. This means bread that is hearth baked and baked the same day you are going to use it (you can buy the bread and freeze it). Combine a few tablespoons of finely crushed garlic with a few tablespoons of extra-virgin olive oil. If you are going to add fresh chopped herbs, add them now.

3. Cut the bread in half lengthwise. With a spoon (not brush, because you want all that garlic on there), spread some of the garlic oil mixture onto the bread. A little bit of oil will go a long way in this instance, and any garlic oil you don't use today, you can use tomorrow in another dish. Sprinkle dried oregano, red pepper flakes and salt on the bread.

4. Put the two pieces back together and place the whole loaf on the middle rack of the oven as it is for about 10 minutes. Take the pieces apart and cook garlic side up for another 10 minutes or until the edges start to brown. To keep the bread warm until company comes, put the loaf back together, cut it into slices and wrap it all together in aluminum foil and place it back in the oven at 150°F.

South African Pap

Servings: 4

INGREDIENTS:

4 cups boiling water
2 cups fine white corn meal
1 tsp. sea salt
fresh ground black pepper

DIRECTIONS:

Pap is the staple dish of South Africa. We would call it grits, but it is much more of a staple in South Africa than it is in the States and it is eaten a bit differently. Pap is a porridge eaten for both breakfast and dinner. This recipe makes a thicker pap eaten with savory dishes and usually enjoyed with Sous* for gravy. For a thinner pap more suitable for breakfast (with fruits, maple syrup or brown sugar) double the amount of water in this recipe and omit the black pepper.

Add the salt to the boiling water. Then add the corn meal all at once. Stir until it comes to boil. Simmer with cover on for about 30 minutes or until tender. Serve warm with Sous* for gravy.

* See Sauces and Dressings

Rice Pilaf

Servings: 4-6

INGREDIENTS:

2 nests vermicelli (Capelli d'Angelo™ Brand)
2 cups rice, any variety (not brown)
½ tsp. sea salt

DIRECTIONS:

Crush the nests of vermicelli between your hands and place them into a dry heated saucepan. While continuously stirring the noodles, toast to a uniform amber color. Add the rice, salt and water. Cook as you would normally cook the rice, adding an extra 1/4 cup of water for the noodles. You can also make this in a rice cooker.

Socca de Nice

Servings: 4

INGREDIENTS:

1 ½ cups chickpea flour
1 ¾ cups water
1 tsp. sea salt
2 Tbs. extra-virgin olive oil
fresh ground black pepper

DIRECTIONS:

Socca is the traditional savory pancake of Nice, France. It is usually sold at small shops and by street vendors in the coastal town. Though simple, I believe it makes a delicious and nutritious appetizer. Chickpea flour can be acquired at any Indian grocery (referred to as gram flour).

1. Preheat oven to 450 °F.

2. Whisk together all the ingredients, making sure to blend in any lumps.

3. Into a well-oiled cast iron pan or skillet, pour some of the batter. You want the thickness to be as it would for a thin pancake. Pour the batter to the edges of the pan. Bake in the oven until golden brown (about 10 minutes). Pop any bubbles that may arise during baking. Broil the top of the pancake for an extraordinary crust. Scrape the pancake off the pan and serve while still hot. It is fine for the pancake to wrinkle up on itself. Garnish with fresh ground black pepper.

VARIATIONS:

You can throw in a handful of fresh rosemary, chopped chives or scallions or your favorite herb before baking. Enjoy with Sous.*

* See Sauces and Dressings

Mamma's Mashed Potatoes

Servings: 4

INGREDIENTS:

4 large Idaho baking potatoes (or any variety you like)
2 Tbs. extra-virgin olive oil
2 Tbs. fresh lemon juice
pinch of dried mint
pinch of cinnamon
pinch of cayenne pepper
sea salt to taste
crushed black pepper

DIRECTIONS:

This is a dish my mom would always make for my baby sister when she refused to eat anything else. It is still one of my sister's favorites and has become one of mine.

1. Preheat oven to 450°F.

2. Wash the potatoes and bake in the oven until fork tender. Do not peel the potatoes. The skin contains the majority of nutrients and flavor. With a fork or potato masher, coarsely mash the potatoes. Add all the ingredients and combine. Adjust salt and black pepper to taste.

Oven-Fried Potatoes

Servings: 4

INGREDIENTS:

4 large potatoes, any variety
2 Tbs. extra-virgin olive oil
sea salt to taste
crushed black pepper

cayenne pepper (optional)
Old Bay Seasoning™ (optional)

DIRECTIONS:

1. Preheat oven to 450°F.

2. Wash the potatoes and slice lengthwise into long ½ inch thick slices. In a bowl, coat the potatoes in olive oil. Add the salt and black pepper. You can also add cayenne pepper, Old Bay Seasoning or any fresh herb or spice you enjoy.

3. Spread potato strips onto a sheet pan lined with aluminum foil. Place the sheet pan on the floor or lowest rack of the oven. When the bottom side of the potatoes has turned a golden brown, place the sheet pan under the broiler to brown the top of the potatoes. Allow them to cool a few minutes before serving. They will taste better than regular French fries and without loads of fat.

Potato Pancakes

Servings: 4

INGREDIENTS:

4 large Idaho baking potatoes OR equivalent in new potatoes
1 medium onion
2 Tbs. corn starch
1 tsp. sea salt to taste
crushed black pepper
fresh thyme or rosemary (optional)
oil cooking spray or extra virgin olive oil

DIRECTIONS:

1. Wash the potatoes, but do not peel. Shred potatoes either with a hand shredder or food processor. Peel and shred the onion as well.

2. Warm up a non-stick skillet over medium heat. To the potatoes, add the cornstarch, salt, pepper and chopped fresh herbs if you like. Mix well and place into a colander. The salt will begin to leech water out of the potatoes, so you want to cook them as soon as possible. The other option is to add the salt while they are cooking.

3. Spray the pan with cooking spray or pour olive oil to just coat the pan. The cooking spray will add considerably less fat to the dish. Cook on one side until golden brown. Turn over and cook on the other side. This dish makes for a delicious breakfast.

Rosemary Garlic Potatoes

Servings: 4

INGREDIENTS:

2 pounds red bliss potatoes (or any small variety you like)
2 Tbs. extra-virgin olive oil
handful of fresh chopped garlic
4 large sprigs fresh rosemary
sea salt to taste
crushed black pepper

DIRECTIONS:

1. Preheat oven to 450°F.

2. Wash the potatoes. Remove rosemary leaves from the stems and chop them very coarsely just one time. Add rosemary, garlic, olive oil, generous sprinkle of salt and black pepper.

3. Spread potatoes onto a sheet pan lined with aluminum foil. Place the sheet pan in the middle of the oven. Cook until potatoes are browned, between 30-40 minutes.

Roasted Garlic Mashed Potatoes

Servings: 4

INGREDIENTS:

4 large Idaho baking potatoes OR about 2 pounds red bliss, new potatoes (or any variety you like)
2 Tbs. extra-virgin olive oil
1 whole head garlic, peeled
sea salt to taste
crushed black pepper
fresh thyme or rosemary (optional)

DIRECTIONS:

1. You can either bake Idaho potatoes or boil two pounds of small red bliss or new potatoes. Wash the potatoes. Bake in the oven at 450°F or boil in pot of salted water until fork tender. Do not peel the potatoes (if you are boiling larger potatoes, you will have to peel them). The skin contains the majority of nutrients and flavor.

2. The following is a quick and easy way to roast garlic. In a clay dish or small sauté pan that is oven safe, pour oil and add all the peeled whole garlic cloves. Cook over low heat until the garlic just starts to brown. You can finish cooking the garlic either on the stovetop or in the oven, whichever is more convenient for you. The garlic cloves are done when they are a uniform light brown color and soft in texture.

3. With a fork or potato masher, coarsely mash the potatoes. Add all the garlic and oil and mash into the potatoes. Throw in a handful of fresh chopped thyme or rosemary, if you like. Adjust salt and black pepper for flavor.

Soups

Black Bean Soup

Servings: 6-8

INGREDIENTS:

1 pound dry black beans
6 cloves fresh garlic, minced
1 medium onion, diced (brunoise)
2 carrots, diced (brunoise)
1 small stalk of celery, diced (brunoise)
1-2 smoked chipotle peppers in adobe, diced
2 ½ Tbs. extra-virgin olive oil
1 tsp. ground coriander
1 tsp. ground cumin
8 cups vegetable stock or water
1/3 cup dry sherry
dried oregano, generous pinch
1 bunch fresh cilantro, minced
1 lime, cut into wedges
sea salt and crushed red pepper to taste

DIRECTIONS:

Soak beans overnight in cold water to cover, and drain before adding to soup. In a 4 quart pot, sauté onions, celery and carrots in olive oil until wilted. Add garlic and cook until it begins to brown. Add spices and chipotle and sauté for 1 minute. Add remainder of ingredients including beans, but excluding sherry, cilantro and lime. Bring mixture to a boil, turn heat down, cover and simmer for 1½ to 2 hours until beans are tender. Add water as needed during cooking to cover the beans. When soup is done, you can purée half the soup and add it back to the remainder. Add sherry and stir. Garnish with cilantro and lime wedges.

Butternut Squash-Apple Bisque

Servings: 6

INGREDIENTS:

1 butternut squash, peeled and cubed
4 tart apples, peeled and cubed
1 medium yellow onion, minced
4 cloves fresh garlic, minced
1 tsp. fresh ginger, grated
1 Tbs. ground coriander
1 Tbs. ground cumin
1 tsp. ground cinnamon
½ tsp. cayenne pepper
fresh sage or tarragon
2 Tbs. extra-virgin olive oil
vegetable broth or water
1 Tbs. real maple syrup
sea salt to taste

Garnish: fresh sage oil

DIRECTIONS:

In a large pot, sauté onions in olive oil until light brown. Add garlic and ginger. Cook until garlic begins to brown. Throw in apples and sauté for 5 minutes. Add spices and fresh herbs and sauté for two minutes. Add butternut squash and sauté for another 5 minutes. Add enough stock or water to just cover the ingredients. Bring to a boil, cover and simmer. Soup is done when squash is soft. Turn heat off, check for seasoning. In a blender, purée the soup. Stir in maple syrup. Garnish each bowl with a thin swirl of fresh sage oil.

Fresh Sage Oil:
Blend a handful of fresh sage with a sprinkle of salt and 2 Tbs. extra-virgin olive oil in a mini food processor.

Curried Sweet Potato Soup

Servings: 4

INGREDIENTS:

3 sweet potatoes, peeled, cubed
1½ cups dry lentils
2 tomatoes, chopped
1 medium yellow onion, minced
6 cloves fresh garlic, minced
1 tsp. grated fresh ginger
1 Tbs. premixed curry powder
1 ½ Tbs. extra-virgin olive oil
6 cups vegetable broth or water
sea salt to taste
crushed red pepper to taste

Garnish: fresh cilantro, minced
        fresh lemon juice

DIRECTIONS:

In a large pot, sauté onions in olive oil until light brown. Add garlic and ginger. Cook until garlic begins to brown. Add tomatoes and cook until they begin to break down. Add curry powder and sauté for one minute. Add lentils, sweet potatoes and broth. Bring the soup to a boil, cover and simmer until lentils are soft. Turn heat off, check for seasoning. Garnish with cilantro and a squeeze of fresh lemon juice.

Five Bean Soup

Servings: 6

INGREDIENTS:

1/3 cup each of dry kidney beans, black beans, navy beans, green split peas and adzuki beans
8 cloves fresh garlic, minced
1 large onion, diced (brunoise)
2 Tbs. extra-virgin olive oil
1 can plum or crushed tomatoes with juice
1 Tbs. ground coriander
1 Tbs. ground cumin
1 tsp. mustard powder
8 cups vegetable stock or water
1 bunch fresh Italian parsley, minced
sea salt and crushed red pepper to taste

DIRECTIONS:

In a 4 quart pot, sauté onions in olive oil until wilted. Add garlic and cook until it begins to brown. Add spices and sauté for 1 minute. Add remainder of ingredients except for parsley. Bring mixture to a boil, turn heat down, cover and simmer for 2 to 2 ½ hours until beans are tender. Add water as needed during cooking to cover the beans. When soup is done, add parsley and stir.

Minestrone

Servings: 6-8

INGREDIENTS:

½ cup each of dry kidney beans, navy beans and black-eye peas
4 carrots, diced (brunoise)
1 large stalk of celery, diced (brunoise)
1 medium onion, diced (brunoise)
2 large white potatoes, diced
2 yellow squash, diced
2 zucchini, diced
½ head white cabbage, chiffonade (fine slice)
5 fresh tomatoes or 1 can plum tomatoes, drained, chopped
6 cloves fresh garlic, minced
2 Tbs. extra-virgin olive oil
6-8 cups vegetable stock or water
½ pound ditalini or orzo pasta
2 bay leaves
fresh oregano, marjoram, thyme and/or basil, chopped or chiffonade
1 bunch fresh Italian parsley, minced
sea salt and crushed red pepper to taste

DIRECTIONS:

Soak the beans overnight and drain. In a pot, cover the beans with water, bring to a boil and continue to boil until they are tender, about 1 hour. Set aside. In a separate 4 quart pot, sauté onions, celery and carrots in olive oil until they start to brown. Add garlic and cook until it begins to brown. Add the potatoes, bay leaves and fresh herbs (use one or all). Sauté for 5 minutes. Add tomatoes and enough stock to cover by at least one inch. Bring to a boil, turn heat down, cover and simmer until potatoes are just tender. Add beans and pasta and continue to cook until pasta is nearly al-dente. Add cabbage and both types of squash. Simmer for a few more minutes until pasta is al-dente and turn heat off. Add parsley and season to taste with salt and pepper.

Miso Soup

Servings: 4

INGREDIENTS:

½ ounce or 15 grams dried wakame (seaweed)
4 cups water
½ pound extra firm silken or regular tofu
3-4 Tbs. red miso paste (or your favorite variety)
scallions, chopped

DIRECTIONS:

1. Soak wakame in 4 cups water for about 15 minutes. Drain the wakame and use the water as the soup stock, about 4 cups. Be sure not to allow any sand into the soup. Bring the stock to a boil.

2. Meanwhile, rinse the wakame and julienne into thin slices. Dice the tofu into ½ inch pieces. When the stock has boiled, add the tofu and wakame. Simmer for about 5 minutes. Turn the burner off. Dissolve the miso (3 or 4 Tbs. depending on how rich a flavor you want) in ½ cup of the stock and stir this mixture into the pot. Make sure the heat is turned off. Garnish with chopped scallions.

Spinach Lentil Soup

Servings: 6-8

INGREDIENTS:

1 pound dry lentils
2 medium yellow onions, sliced
2 pounds fresh spinach
2 fresh lemons
3 quarts (12 cups) vegetable broth or water
8 cloves fresh garlic, crushed
2 Tbs. extra-virgin olive oil
4 Tbs. sumac (optional)
sea salt to taste
crushed red pepper to taste

Garnish: Toasted pita

DIRECTIONS:

1. In at least a 4 quart pot, add lentils and broth or water. The amount of liquid is not exact. For a thicker soup use less water and vice versa. Bring this mixture to a boil and cook until the lentils are tender. Meanwhile you can prepare the rest of the soup.

2. In a skillet, sauté onions in olive oil until light brown and set aside. When lentils are done cooking, turn heat down to medium and add the cooked onions, raw garlic, juice of two lemons and sumac. Sumac is a crimson colored sour herb taken from the sumac plant. It is used in dishes to complement the acid of lemon juice. Allow the soup to cook for another 10 minutes so the garlic flavor really comes out and then turn the burner off. Add all of the spinach in small increments because it will wilt as you add it. Lastly, season with salt and pepper to taste.

3. This soup can be enjoyed hot or cold and is traditionally eaten with toasted pita (instead of crackers).

VARIATIONS:

In addition you may add 2 large potatoes, peeled, cut into half inch cubes. Add the potatoes after the lentils have cooked and before you add the remaining ingredients. You may also use Swiss chard instead of spinach.

Vegetable Miso Soup

Servings: 6

INGREDIENTS:

½ ounce or 15 grams dried wakame (seaweed)
6 cups water
½ pound extra-firm silken or regular tofu
2 tsp. sesame oil
1 small onion or scallion, chopped
2 cloves fresh garlic, chopped
1 Tbs. fresh grated ginger
½ cup chopped carrots
½ cup chopped daikon (radish) (optional)
1 cup mushrooms, sliced
1 cup Chinese cabbage, chopped
1 cup snow peas, cut in half
4 Tbs. red miso paste
scallions, chopped, to garnish
bean sprouts to garnish

DIRECTIONS:

1. Soak wakame in 6 cups water for about 15 minutes. Drain the wakame and use the water as the soup stock. Be sure not to allow any sand into the soup.

2. Rinse the wakame and julienne into thin pieces. Dice the tofu into ½ inch pieces. Prepare the remainder of the vegetables as well. In a large pot, sauté the onion, garlic and ginger until they start to brown. Add the carrots, daikon and mushrooms. Cook until they begin to caramelize. Add the stock and bring to a boil. When the stock has boiled, add the tofu and wakame. Simmer for about 5 minutes. Turn burner off. Add the cabbage and snow peas. Dissolve the miso in 1 cup of the stock and stir this mixture into the pot. Make sure the heat is turned off. Garnish with chopped scallions and bean sprouts.

Vegetable Soup

Servings: 6-8

INGREDIENTS:

6 carrots, sliced
1 large stalk of celery, sliced
3 large white potatoes, cubed
3 yellow squash, cubed
3 zucchini, cubed
½ head white cabbage, cut into 1 inch pieces
5 fresh tomatoes or 1 can plum tomatoes, drained, chopped
6 cloves fresh garlic, minced
1 medium onion, diced (brunoise)
2 Tbs. extra-virgin olive oil
6-8 cups vegetable stock or water
2 bay leaves
dried oregano, generous pinch
1 bunch fresh Italian parsley, minced
sea salt, black pepper and crushed red pepper to taste

DIRECTIONS:

In a 4 quart pot, sauté onions in olive oil until wilted. Add garlic and cook until it begins to brown. Add the potatoes, carrots, celery, bay leaves and oregano. Sauté for 5 minutes. Add tomatoes and stock to cover vegetables by at least one inch. Bring to a boil, turn heat down, cover and simmer until potatoes are just tender. Add cabbage and both types of squash. Simmer for a few more minutes and turn heat off. Add parsley and season with salt and pepper.

Sauces and Dressings

Balsamic Vinaigrette

INGREDIENTS:

1 part balsamic vinegar
1 part extra-virgin olive oil
1/24 part salt
crushed black pepper to taste
fresh crushed garlic, pinch (optional)
dried oregano, pinch (optional)
fresh thyme, pinch (optional)
fresh basil, pinch (optional)

Measurements: 3 teaspoons = 1 Tablespoon.

DIRECTIONS:

Recipes for dressings work better in proportions so that you can make as much as you want. For example, if you wanted to make ½ cup of balsamic vinaigrette, you would use: 4 Tbs. vinegar, 4 Tbs. olive oil, and ½ tsp. salt. Buy the best balsamic vinegar you can afford. This means the older the vinegar, the more expensive it will be, but also the sweeter and more complex the flavor will be. You can get a pretty decent bottle for about ten dollars. Use your taste and judgment for the remainder of the ingredients. I love garlic, so I like to use garlic in almost everything. Combine all ingredients in a blender or mini food processor. Blend until you have a homogenous mixture. You can also use a hand whisk; however, this does not do as good a job emulsifying the ingredients. This dressing will keep indefinitely if refrigerated.

Dijon Mustard Vinaigrette

INGREDIENTS:

½ part French Dijon Mustard
1 ½ parts fresh lemon juice
2 parts extra-virgin olive oil
crushed black pepper to taste
dried oregano, pinch (optional)
fresh thyme, pinch (optional)
fresh basil, pinch (optional)

Measurements: 3 teaspoons = 1 Tablespoon.

DIRECTIONS:

Recipes for dressings work better in proportions so that you can make as much as you
want. For example, if you wanted to make ½ cup of Dijon Mustard Vinaigrette, you
would use: 1 Tbs. mustard, 3 Tbs. lemon juice and 4 Tbs. olive oil. Buy a good quality
French Dijon mustard that is imported from France. This will make a big difference in
the quality of the dressing. Use your taste and judgment for the remainder of the
ingredients. For this dressing, it depends what I have in my salad, and I adjust the herbs
accordingly. Combine all ingredients in a blender or mini food processor. Blend until
you have a homogenous mixture. You can also use a hand whisk; however, this does not
do as good a job emulsifying the ingredients. This dressing will keep indefinitely if
refrigerated.

Lemon Vinaigrette

INGREDIENTS:

1 part fresh lemon juice
1 part extra-virgin olive oil
1/24 part sea salt
crushed black pepper to taste
fresh crushed garlic, pinch (optional)

Measurements: 3 teaspoons = 1 Tablespoon.

DIRECTIONS:

Recipes for dressings work better in proportions so that you can make as much as you want. For example, if you wanted to make ½ cup of Lemon Vinaigrette, you would use: 4 Tbs. lemon juice, 4 Tbs. olive oil and ½ tsp salt. If you use garlic in this recipe, it is the traditional Lebanese Salad dressing. Growing up, we ate this essentially on every salad, except tabouli. I have grown to like this dressing without garlic, but try it out and see what you like. Combine all ingredients in a blender or mini food processor. Blend until you have a homogenous mixture. You can also use a hand whisk; however, this does not do as good a job emulsifying the ingredients. This dressing will keep indefinitely if refrigerated.

VARIATION:

Fresh Lemon Vinaigrette with Garlic. Substitute fresh orange juice for ½ of the lemon juice and add a pinch of fresh garlic.

Miso-Ginger Dressing

INGREDIENTS:

2 parts red or mild miso
2 parts seasoned rice wine vinegar
1 part fresh lemon juice
3 parts extra-virgin olive oil
½ part dark sesame oil
¼ part soy sauce
1 part fresh grated ginger or ginger powder
1 part water
crushed black pepper to taste

Measurements: 3 teaspoons = 1 Tablespoon.

DIRECTIONS:

Recipes for dressings work better in proportions so that you can make as much as you want. For example, if you wanted to make about ½ cup of this Miso-Ginger Dressing, each part would be equivalent to one tablespoon. This is one of my favorite salad dressings. Milder miso (fermented soybean paste) works better than darker miso for this recipe, but you can use any variety you like. I generally use everything fresh, but I have found that powdered ginger is one of those ingredients that does well in recipes when used to replace fresh ginger, especially in this recipe, since dried ginger loses a lot of the bite that fresh ginger has. Combine all ingredients in a blender or mini food processor. Blend until you have a homogenous mixture. A hand whisk really would not work well in this case. This dressing will keep indefinitely if refrigerated.

Sumac Dressing

INGREDIENTS:

1 part fresh lemon juice
1 part dry sumac
2 parts extra-virgin olive oil
1/24 part sea salt
crushed black pepper to taste
fresh crushed garlic, pinch

Measurements: 3 teaspoons = 1 Tablespoon.

DIRECTIONS:

Recipes for dressings work better in proportions so that you can make as much as you want. For example, if you wanted to make ½ cup of this Sumac Dressing, you would use: 2 Tbs. lemon juice, 2 Tbs. sumac, 4 Tbs. olive oil, a pinch or so of garlic and ¼ tsp salt. This is the dressing traditionally used for Fattoush, a famous Lebanese salad which, I promise, will be the best you've ever eaten. It is good to use at least a little bit of garlic in this recipe. Combine all ingredients in a blender or mini food processor. Blend until you have a homogenous mixture. You can also use a hand whisk; however, this does not do as good a job emulsifying the ingredients. This dressing will keep indefinitely if refrigerated.

Tahini Dressing (Taratoor)

INGREDIENTS:

2 parts tahini (sesame seed paste)
2 parts fresh lemon juice
3 parts water
1/24 part sea salt
fresh crushed garlic, pinch

Measurements: 3 teaspoons = 1 Tablespoon.

DIRECTIONS:

Recipes for dressings work better in proportions so that you can make as much as you want. For example, if you wanted to make about ½ cup of tahini sauce you would use: 4 Tbs. tahini, 4 Tbs. lemon juice, 6 Tbs. water and ¼ tsp salt. Garlic makes a difference in this recipe, so it really is not optional. Tahini sauce or "taratoor" as it is known in Arabic is the traditional dressing for falafel. You can also use this dressing for salads. Combine all ingredients in a blender or mini food processor. Blend until you have a homogenous mixture. You can use a hand whisk; however, this does not do as good a job emulsifying the ingredients. This dressing will keep indefinitely if refrigerated.

White Wine Vinaigrette

INGREDIENTS:

1 part white or red wine vinegar
1 part extra-virgin olive oil
1/24 part sea salt
crushed black pepper to taste
fresh crushed garlic, pinch (optional)
fresh thyme (optional)
fresh oregano (optional)
fresh sage (optional)

Measurements: 3 teaspoons = 1 Tablespoon.

DIRECTIONS:

Recipes for dressings work better in proportions so that you can make as much as you want. For example, if you wanted to make ½ cup of this dressing, you would use: 4 Tbs. wine, 4 Tbs. olive oil and 1/2 tsp. salt. This is your basic Italian salad dressing. Depending on what you are in the mood for, you can add any or all of the optional ingredients. Combine all ingredients in a blender or mini food processor. Blend until you have a homogenous mixture. You can also use a hand whisk; however, this does not do as good a job emulsifying the ingredients. This dressing will keep indefinitely if refrigerated.

Marinara Sauce (Basic "Gravy")

INGREDIENTS:

2 28-oz. cans San Marzano™ Plum Tomatoes
1 medium yellow onion, diced
8 cloves fresh crushed garlic
2 Tbs. extra-virgin olive oil
fresh basil
dried oregano
sea salt to taste
crushed red pepper to taste
real maple syrup (optional, if needed)

DIRECTIONS:

1. First, you can make this sauce chunky or smooth, depending on your taste. I like pasta sauce smooth with just a little bit of texture. You can use the drained canning juice from other recipes to make this sauce as well. The best thing to do is to crush the tomatoes using a manual food mill. If you don't have one, use a food processor or blender. I would not use canned crushed tomatoes. They just don't have the flavor of a whole plum tomato. Ideally you want to use your garden grown plum tomatoes (peeled, by scalding in boiling water for a minute) or San Marzano tomatoes grown in Italy (they are more expensive, but also much sweeter and more flavorful than the tomatoes grown in California).

2. In hot sauce pan over medium heat, sauté onions in the olive oil until translucent. Add the garlic and cook until garlic just starts to brown. Add a handful of fresh whole basil leaf and a generous pinch of dried oregano rubbed between your fingers. Cook for just a few seconds. Add the crushed tomatoes and salt. Bring the sauce to a boil, then lower heat to simmer. Cover the sauce and cook until you have the desired thickness (at least 45 minutes). Taste the sauce for salt and add some crushed red pepper flakes and a touch of maple syrup if the sauce is not sweet enough for you.

3. This sauce goes well on pasta or for lasagna and can be refrigerated/frozen until it smells or tastes bad.

Pizza Sauce

INGREDIENTS:

2 28-oz. cans San Marzano™ Plum Tomatoes
4 cloves fresh crushed garlic
2 Tbs. extra-virgin olive oil
fresh basil
dried oregano
sea salt to taste
crushed red pepper to taste
fresh oregano, fresh marjoram (optional)

DIRECTIONS:

1. Just like the pasta sauce, you can make this sauce chunky or smooth, depending on your taste. I like to make this pizza sauce smooth (for a chunky pizza sauce, I prefer the Roasted Garlic Pizza Sauce) with just a little bit of texture. The best thing to do is to crush the tomatoes (be sure to squeeze all the juice out of the tomatoes and drain off all the juice using a strainer; you can use this to make pasta sauce later) using a manual food mill. If you don't have one, use a food processor or blender. And again, I would almost never use canned crushed tomatoes. They just don't have the flavor of a whole plum tomato. Ideally you want to use your garden grown plum tomatoes (peeled, by scalding in boiling water for a minute) or San Marzano tomatoes grown in Italy (they are more expensive, but also much sweeter and more flavorful than the tomatoes grown in California).

2. This sauce is not cooked. Using a hand whisk, simply combine the crushed tomatoes, garlic, olive oil, salt, a handful of torn basil leaves, dried oregano and as much red pepper as you like. If you want your sauce to be a bit more aromatic, add some roughly chopped fresh oregano and/or marjoram. Your sauce is ready to use.

Roasted Garlic Pizza Sauce

INGREDIENTS:

4 28-oz. cans San Marzano™ plum tomatoes
one whole head garlic, peeled
3 Tbs. extra-virgin olive oil
fresh basil
dried oregano
sea salt to taste
crushed red pepper to taste

fresh oregano, fresh marjoram (optional)

DIRECTIONS:

1. This is my pizza sauce of preference because it can stand alone on a pizza. In other words you don't any other ingredients to make the pizza taste good. This sauce, I always make chunky and the basic difference is adding a whole lot of cooked garlic instead of raw garlic. In this case, you don't want to crush the tomatoes. Squeeze the juice out of tomatoes and drain off all the juice using a strainer. You can use this juice to make pasta sauce later on. Once you have done this, mash the tomatoes between your fingers until you have chunks and stringy pieces. Ideally you want to use your garden grown plum tomatoes (peeled, by scalding in boiling water for a minute) or San Marzano tomatoes grown in Italy (they are more expensive, but also much sweeter and more flavorful than the tomatoes grown in California).

2. In a sauté pan over low heat, pour oil and add all the peeled whole garlic cloves immediately. This is a quick and easy way to roast garlic. Since you are going to use the olive oil, you may as well flavor it with the garlic. Cook the garlic over low heat until all the garlic cloves are just lightly browned and soft in texture. Immediately turn off heat. Add all the garlic and oil to the tomatoes. Add salt, a handful of torn basil leaves, dried oregano and as much red pepper as you like. If you want your sauce to be a bit more aromatic, add some roughly chopped fresh oregano and/or marjoram. Your sauce is ready to use.

Sous

INGREDIENTS:

1 large onion, finely chopped
5-6 fresh medium sized tomatoes or 8 plum tomatoes, skinned, roughly chopped
2 cloves fresh minced garlic
2 Tbs. extra-virgin olive oil
sea salt to taste
fresh ground black pepper to taste

DIRECTIONS:

This is the traditional gravy eaten with South African pap. I also like to dip Socca* in it.

In a sauce pan over medium heat, sauté the onions until translucent. Add the garlic and cook for a few minutes. Add the tomatoes and salt. Simmer until tomatoes have broken down and sauce has thickened.

*See Appetizers and Side Dishes

Asian Dipping Sauce

INGREDIENTS:

3 parts rice wine vinegar
2 parts soy sauce
1 part sugar
½ part fresh sliced garlic
¼ part fresh grated ginger
¼ part sesame oil
crushed red chili peppers
chopped scallions

DIRECTIONS:

This sauce is meant as a dipping sauce for dumplings or scallion pancakes. It also makes a great marinade. It is pretty much equivalent to a teriyaki sauce. I wrote this recipe in proportions so that you can make as much as you want. For example, if you wanted to make about 2/3 cup of this sauce, you would use: 6 Tbs. vinegar, 4 Tbs. soy sauce, 2 Tbs. sugar, 1 Tbs. garlic, ½ Tbs. ginger and ½ Tbs. sesame oil.

1. In hot sauce pan, sauté garlic, ginger and chilies in sesame oil. Use chilies according to your taste.

2. Add the remainder of the ingredients and cook just until the sugar is dissolved. Garnish with chopped scallions.

3. To use as a marinade, chop the garlic instead of slicing it.

Nana Saul's Barbecue Sauce

INGREDIENTS:

4 cubes vegetable boullion
2 cups boiling water
1 cup ketchup
4 Tbs. dried onion flakes
4 Tbs. lemon juice
2 Tbs. extra-virgin olive oil
2 tsp. dried mustard
2 tsp. dark brown sugar
cayenne pepper to taste

DIRECTIONS:

1. Dissolve boullion cubes in boiling water. Once dissolved, add remaining ingredients and bring to a boil.

2. Simmer until sauce has thickened to desired consistency, at least 30 minutes.

Spicy Garlic Sauce

INGREDIENTS:

3 cups crushed pineapple with juice
1/3 cup orange juice concentrate
2/3 cup sweet soy sauce
2/3 cup soy sauce
1 whole head garlic, peeled, crushed
1/3 cup fresh or ½ cup pickled ginger (rinsed), finely chopped
2 Tbs. extra-virgin olive oil
10 dried red hot chili peppers, roughly crushed

DIRECTIONS:

1. Combine all ingredients except garlic, ginger and chilies in a food processor and blend until smooth.

2. In hot sauce pan, sauté garlic, ginger and chilies in olive oil until they just start to wilt. You do not want to brown the garlic. Quickly add the ingredients from step 1.

3. Bring to a boil and cook for 15 minutes.

4. Refrigerate indefinitely. This sauce makes a wonderful marinade.

Salads

Arugula Salad

Servings: 4

INGREDIENTS:

1 ½-2 pounds arugula or baby arugula
2 Tbs. pine nuts
1 roasted red pepper
handful of sun-dried tomatoes
sea salt to taste
crushed black pepper to taste
crushed red pepper, pinch

4 Tbs. Balsamic, Fresh Lemon or White Wine Vinaigrette*

DIRECTIONS:

Don't be afraid to try new vegetables. Arugula is one of the most underappreciated greens, in my opinion. It is a bit on the peppery side, but it is loaded with flavor and nutrients.

1. Wash and dry the arugula as necessary and put into the largest bowl you own. If you are using large leaves, cut them in half.

2. I usually use canned roasted red peppers. They are almost as good as the fresh roasted ones, but without all the work. If you want fresh roasted red peppers, see the recipe for Hot Ajvar. Slice the peppers into thin strips and add to the greens.

3. I recommend using sun-dried tomatoes that are not in oil. The extra oil is not at all necessary. Good quality sun-dried tomatoes are not completely dry either. They have some moisture to them and should be edible without pre-soaking. Slice the tomatoes into thin strips. If they are very dry, soak in warm water for ½ hour first.

4. In a dry skillet over low heat, toast the pine nuts to a light brown color. Add to the salad. Drizzle on your favorite dressing (I alternate between lemon and balsamic), salt, pepper and toss. Sprinkle some crushed red pepper for an extra kick.

*See Sauces and Dressings

Asian Noodle Salad

Servings: 4

INGREDIENTS:

1 ½ pounds broccoli
½ pound snow peas
1 fresh sweet red pepper
handful fresh Thai basil, julienned
2 Tbs. black sesame seeds
sea salt to taste
crushed black pepper to taste
hot chili sauce (Sriracha™ brand)
1 pound dry thin linguine
4-6 Tbs. Miso Ginger Vinaigrette*

DIRECTIONS:

1. Cut the broccoli into large bite size pieces. Cut the snow peas in half on a diagonal. Slice the carrots on a diagonal as well. You want to blanch or steam these veggies until the broccoli is a bright green color. To blanch, place the veggies into a pot of boiling, salted water. Blanch the carrots with the broccoli. When the broccoli turns a bright green, both the carrots and broccoli are done. Drain the veggies and drop into a bowl of ice water until they are cool. Do the same with the snow peas. They will cook faster than the broccoli. Be sure to drain the veggies well once they have cooled.

2. Thinly slice the peppers. If you cannot find Thai basil (it has a purplish hue to it), then use lemon basil and if you can't find that, use regular basil.

3. Cook the pasta until it is just al-dente and place under running cold water until cool.

4. Combine all the veggies and pasta. Add the basil and the vinaigrette. I like to add a small amount of chili sauce to spice things up a bit. In my opinion, Sriracha makes the best Asian hot sauce. Adjust salt and pepper to taste. Refrigerate until you are ready to eat.

*See Sauces and Dressings

Baby Beet Salad

Servings: 4

INGREDIENTS:

2 pounds baby beets
1/3 cup sliced almonds
sea salt to taste
crushed black pepper to taste
fresh orange juice
fresh tarragon (optional)

3-4 Tbs. Fresh Lemon Vinaigrette*, with garlic, see below

DIRECTIONS:

1. Cut the stems off the beets and wash them. Place them in a pot, cover with water, add salt and bring to a boil. Cook until they are just fork tender (the beets should hold their shape completely, even when cut). When they are done cooking, run under cold water over them or place them in an ice bath until cool. The skin should come right off. Slice the beets into halves or quarters.

2. To make the vinaigrette, use the recipe for fresh lemon vinaigrette, but substitute fresh orange juice for ½ of the lemon juice and add a pinch of fresh garlic.

3. In a dry skillet over low heat, toast the almonds to a light brown color. Add to the salad. Add some fresh torn tarragon leaves and the dressing. Mix the ingredients well. Adjust salt and pepper to taste.

*See Sauces and Dressings

Fattoush

Servings: 4

INGREDIENTS:

1 ½-2 pounds mixed salad greens of your choice, see below
1 package grape tomatoes
1 pound, red bliss potatoes
1 fresh green pepper, sliced
10 radishes, sliced finely
1 bunch fresh Italian parsley, whole leaves
1 bunch fresh mint, julienned
1 medium red onion or sweet onion or 3 green onions (optional), sliced
2 large thin Lebanese pitas, toasted
sea salt to taste
crushed black pepper to taste

6-8 Tbs. Sumac Dressing (See Sauces and Dressings)

DIRECTIONS:

This is the mother of all salads. It is a meal all by itself. You are not limited to just the ingredients listed, obviously. This salad is traditionally eaten during the summertime when there is an abundance of everything. Feel free to include any vegetables you would like.

1. Fresh greens. I like to use mesclun mixed greens, but you can use any variety you like. (I would never recommend iceberg lettuce in anything you eat.) Some recommendations include Boston lettuce, red lettuce, green lettuce, escarole, radicchio, endive, frizze, baby spinach, baby arugula, chicory and baby dandelion. Wash and dry the greens as necessary and put into the largest bowl you own.

2. Wash the potatoes and put them in a pot; cover with water and add salt. Bring to a boil and cook until the potatoes are tender, but not mushy, 15 to 25 minutes. The potatoes should hold their shape completely, even when cut. When they are done cooking, run them under cold water or place them in an ice bath until cool. This is called shocking the vegetables and it will stop the cooking. Slice each potato into halves or quarters. Add to the greens. Add the remainder of the vegetables.

3. Toast the two large pita in either a toaster oven or a regular oven until they are medium brown. When cooled, break pita up into small bite size pieces with your hands. Add to salad.

4. Add 6 to 8 Tbs. of salad dressing. The pita will soak up some of the dressing, so the amount varies. Season with salt and pepper as needed. Enjoy fresh.

Garden Salad

Servings: 4

INGREDIENTS:

1 – 1½ pounds mixed salad greens of your choice, see below
2 large tomatoes, sliced or 1 package grape tomatoes
½ English cucumber sliced
1 sweet red pepper, sliced
2 carrots, thinly sliced
6-8 radishes, finely sliced
handful fresh mint leaves (optional)
sea salt to taste
crushed black pepper to taste

See Vinaigrettes for Your favorite Vinaigrette salad dressing*.

DIRECTIONS:

This is your standard, everyday salad. You are never limited to just the ingredients listed. Use your imagination. Most importantly, use the best ingredients that are available and affordable to you. Here are a few words on salad greens. Don't ever buy iceberg lettuce. It has neither flavor nor nutritional value. I like to use mesclun mixed greens, but you can use any variety you like. Some recommendations include Boston lettuce, red lettuce, green lettuce, escarole, endive, radicchio, frizze, baby spinach, baby arugula, chicory and baby dandelion. Wash and dry the greens as necessary. Prepackaged mixes are fine too, as long as they don't contain iceberg lettuce.

*See Sauces and Dressings

Italian Pasta Salad

Servings: 4

INGREDIENTS:

1 pound broccoli
1 pound cauliflower
1 fresh sweet red pepper
1 fresh sweet green pepper
1 can artichoke hearts
½ cup green olives, any variety
handful fresh basil, julienned
sea salt to taste
dried oregano
crushed black pepper to taste
1 pound tricolor spiral pasta
4-6 Tbs. Fresh Lemon Vinaigrette with garlic*

DIRECTIONS:

1. Cut the broccoli and cauliflower into large bite size pieces. You want to either blanch or steam these veggies until the broccoli is a bright green color. To blanch, place the veggies into a pot of boiling, salted water. When the broccoli turns a bright green and is just fork tender, drain the veggies and drop into a bowl of ice water until they are cool.

2. Thinly slice the peppers and green olives. Drain the artichoke hearts and cut into quarters.

3. Cook the pasta until it is just al-dente and place under running cold water until cool.

4. Combine all the veggies and pasta. Add the basil and a generous sprinkling of dried oregano. Add the lemon vinaigrette. Be generous with the amount of garlic. It really suits this dish well. Adjust salt and pepper to taste. Refrigerate until you are ready to eat.

*See Sauces and Dressings

Potato Salad

Servings: 4

INGREDIENTS:

2 pounds red bliss potatoes (or any small variety you like)
2 medium tomatoes
1 medium red onion or sweet onion or 3 spring onions (scallions)
pinch of dried mint or handful of fresh chopped mint
handful of fresh chopped Italian parsley
sea salt to taste
crushed black pepper to taste
4 Tbs. Lemon Vinaigrette*

DIRECTIONS:

1. Wash the potatoes and place in a pot; cover with water and add salt. Bring to a boil and cook until the potatoes are tender, but not mushy, 15 to 25 minutes. The potatoes should hold their shape completely, even when cut. When they are done cooking, run them under cold water or place them in an ice bath until cool. This is called shocking the vegetables and it will stop the cooking.   If you are using larger potatoes, you will have to skin them. Slice each potato into halves or quarters.

2. To the potatoes add the sliced onion or chopped green onion, sliced tomatoes, and the remainder of the ingredients. Add salt and pepper as desired. I find this salad is best eaten fresh. When onions and tomatoes sit around in a salad overnight, they both wilt and the onions become too fragrant.

*See Sauces and Dressings

Spinach Salad

Servings: 4

INGREDIENTS:

1 ½-2 pounds baby spinach or regular spinach
1 package white button mushrooms
sun-dried tomatoes, handful
2 medium red onions sliced
2 tsp. extra-virgin olive oil
¼ cup water
1 cup Homemade Croutons*
sea salt to taste
crushed black pepper to taste
crushed red pepper, pinch

3-4 Tbs. Balsamic Vinaigrette**

DIRECTIONS:

1. Wash and dry the spinach as necessary and put into a large bowl. If you are using regular spinach, discard the large stems and tear the leaves into smaller pieces.

2. Do not wash the mushrooms. In fact, you should never wash mushrooms. Gently brush off any "dirt." Slice the mushrooms and throw them into the salad.

3. I recommend using sun-dried tomatoes that are not in oil. The extra oil is not at all necessary. Good quality sun-dried tomatoes are not completely dry either. They have some moisture to them and should be edible without pre-soaking. Slice the tomatoes into thin strips. If they are very dry, soak in warm water for ½ hour first.

4. In a skillet over low heat add the oil and onions with a dash of salt. To caramelize the onions, once they have wilted and just started to brown, add about ¼ cup of water and cover. Cook until the onions are a uniform light brown, stirring occasionally.

5. To assemble the salad, mix the spinach and mushrooms, drizzle on the balsamic dressing, salt and pepper; toss. Top off the salad with the warm onions and croutons. Sprinkle some crushed red pepper for an extra kick.

*See Appetizers and Side Dishes

**See Sauces and Dressings

Tabouli

Servings: 6

INGREDIENTS:

6 bunches flat leaf (Italian) parsley, washed, allowed to dry
3 ripe medium size tomatoes
1 small onion
½ cup fine grain whole wheat bulgur, soaked in 1 cup warm water
2 Tbs. extra-virgin olive oil
juice of 3 fresh lemons
½ bunch of fresh mint (optional)
1 tsp. salt to taste
Fine dash of allspice

DIRECTIONS:

1. Julienne parsley as finely as possible. Do not use a food processor to do this. You must use a sharp utility knife. Take your time and be careful. My mother does this better than anyone I know, but she has had years of practice. Finely dice the tomatoes and onion.

2. To the ingredients from step 1 add the soaked bulgur wheat, lemon juice, olive oil, salt, allspice and mint if desired. Be sure the bulgur is not crunchy and drain off any excess water. Mix the salad well, using your hands and rubbing the ingredients together between your fingers. Adjust the salt, lemon juice and olive oil according to your taste.

3. When fresh pomegranate is available, it makes an excellent addition to this salad. Just crumble the seeds into the salad.

Breads & Pizzas

Authentic Neapolitan Pizza Dough

INGREDIENTS:

For 8 Pizzas

1 2/3 cups "00" double zero flour
5 cups Hi-Gluten (Pizza) flour
OR use 6 2/3 cups Unbleached Bread Flour
2 tsp. instant yeast
2 tsp. sea salt
3 cups warm water (about 90°F)

For 4 Pizzas

5/6 cup "00" double zero flour (about 7 oz.)
2 ½ cups Hi-Gluten (Pizza) flour
OR use 3 1/3 cups Unbleached Bread Flour
1 tsp. instant yeast
1 tsp. sea salt
1.5 cups warm water (about 90°F)

DIRECTIONS:

1. In the bowl of a stand mixer (or if you are doing this by hand, the biggest bowl you have), dissolve the yeast and salt in the water. Let stand 10 minutes. Meanwhile you can measure out the flour and mix together the two types of flours if you are using both types.

2. Add all the flour at once. Turn mixer to lowest speed until dough becomes soft and silky. Work for another five mutes. By hand do the same thing and once soft and silky work for no more than 10 minutes. This dough has fairly high water content and may tend to stick a bit. Be sure to flour all your working surfaces well. In a bowl, cover the dough with plastic wrap and then a towel. Allow to rise until double in size, about 1 ½ hours.

3. Once dough has doubled in size, divide into the appropriate number of pieces (either 4 or 8). Work into smooth balls. Lay out dough balls on a sheet pan, cover with plastic wrap and a towel. Allow to rise for at least 2 hours. ½ hour before you are ready to make the pizzas, preheat your oven with the baking stone inside at 450°F.

4. Once the dough has rested for the second time, you are ready to make the pizzas. On a well floured surface begin to flatten the dough ball with your fingertips beginning from the inside out and moving in a circular fashion to create a thicker crust at the edges. You can now stretch the dough by dangling it from your fists or fingertips and moving it in a circular fashion. This will take some practice. You can also try tossing the pizzas.

Using your fists, again, cross your hands one over the other with the pizza dangling from your knuckles. With a quick tossing motion uncross your hands, in the process tossing the pizza into the air, spinning it and stretching it out in circular manner. Another option is to use a pin to roll out the pizzas. Pizza should be thin in the middle and thicker as you move out. Place the pizza on a floured peel (you can use a piece of cardboard if you don't have a peel).

5. You can bake the pizzas with nothing on them, and freeze them to use for a quick meal later on or you can bake the pizzas with the toppings for a fresh meal. Recipe ideas for pizzas follow.

Pizza Artichoke

Servings: 4

INGREDIENTS:

1 recipe Pizza Dough (4 pizzas)
1 recipe Roasted Garlic Pizza Sauce*
1 can artichoke hearts
2 roasted red peppers, fresh or canned
2 cloves fresh garlic, minced
fresh marjoram, thyme or oregano, chopped
extra-virgin olive oil
sea salt

DIRECTIONS:

1. Once the dough has proofed (risen) for the second time and your oven with the baking stone is preheated to 450°F, you are ready to bake the pizzas.

2. Slice each artichoke heart into six pieces. Slice the red peppers into thin strips. Add the garlic, fresh chopped herbs and a light drizzle of olive oil with sprinkle of salt. Toss well and set aside until they are ready to use.

3. On a well floured surface begin to flatten the dough ball with your fingertips beginning from the inside out and moving in a circular fashion to create a thicker crust at the edges. You can now stretch the dough by dangling it from your fists or fingertips and moving in a circular fashion. This will take some practice. You can also try tossing the pizzas. Using your fists, again, cross your hands one over the other with the pizza dangling from your knuckles. With a quick tossing motion uncross your hands, in the process tossing the pizza into the air, spinning it and stretching it out in circular manner. Another option is to use a pin to roll out the pizzas. Pizza should be thin in the middle and thicker as you move out. Place the pizza on a floured peel (you can use a piece of cardboard if you don't have a peel).

4. Spread a thin layer of the sauce on the dough. I don't like to use too much because it makes the pizza soggy after it has cooked. Spread a generous portion of the mixed artichoke hearts and peppers.

5. Gently slide the pizza off the peel and onto the stone. If your peel is floured adequately, the pizza should slide right off. Bake until the bottom of the crust is a golden brown, 5-8 minutes. Place it under the broiler for a minute to brown the top of the crust.

*See Sauces and Dressings

Pizza Ensalata

Servings: 4

INGREDIENTS:

1 recipe Pizza Dough (4 pizzas)
1 recipe Roasted Garlic Pizza Sauce or regular Pizza Sauce*
1-1 ½ pounds salad greens
2 roasted red peppers, fresh or canned
6-8 Tb. Balsamic, Fresh Lemon or White Wine Vinaigrette*
fresh basil leaves
dried oregano
extra-virgin olive oil

DIRECTIONS:

1. Once the dough has proofed (risen) for the second time and your oven with the baking stone is preheated to 450°F, you are ready to bake the pizzas.

2. On a well floured surface begin to flatten the dough ball with your fingertips beginning from the inside out and moving in a circular fashion to create a thicker crust at the edges. You can now stretch the dough by dangling it from your fists or fingertips and moving in a circular fashion. This will take some practice. You can also try tossing the pizzas. Using your fists, again, cross your hands one over the other with the pizza dangling from your knuckles. With a quick tossing motion uncross your hands, in the process tossing the pizza into the air, spinning it and stretching it out in circular manner. Another option is to use a pin to roll out the pizzas. Pizza should be thin in the middle and thicker as you move out. Place the pizza on a floured peel (you can use a piece of cardboard if you don't have a peel).

3. Lay out some fresh torn basil leaves onto the pizza. Spread a thin layer of the sauce on top of the basil. I don't like to use too much because it makes the pizza soggy after it has cooked. Sprinkle some dried oregano and very light drizzle of olive oil.

4. Gently slide the pizza off the peel and onto the stone. If your peel is floured adequately, the pizza should slide right off. Bake until the bottom of the crust is a golden brown, 5-8 minutes. Place it under the broiler for a minute to brown the top of the crust.

5. While the pizzas are baking, you can make the salad. Use any variety of greens or premixed prepackaged salads, but don't use anything that has iceberg lettuce in it. Iceberg lettuce lends neither flavor nor nutritional value. Slice the red peppers into thin strips and add to the greens. Add salad dressing and mix well. Any of the vinaigrettes recommended above go well with this pizza, so mix and match.

6. When the pizzas are all baked, place a heaping mound of salad right on top of the sauce. Eat with your hands (preferably) or with a knife and fork.

*See Sauces and Dressings

Pizza Fungi

Servings: 4

INGREDIENTS:

1 recipe Pizza Dough (4 pizzas)
1 recipe Roasted Garlic Pizza Sauce or regular Pizza Sauce*
½ pound crimini mushrooms
½ pound shitake mushrooms
fresh marjoram, thyme or oregano, chopped
dried oregano
extra-virgin olive oil
soy cheese (non-dairy) optional

DIRECTIONS:

1. Once the dough has proofed (risen) for the second time and your oven with the baking stone is preheated to 450°F, you are ready to bake the pizzas.

2. To prepare the topping, slice the crimini mushrooms and cut the shitake mushrooms in half. You can use any variety of wild mushroom (chanterelle, porcini etc...) you like. Shitakes are the least expensive and most widely available. Criminis are cheap and can be found everywhere. In a hot non-stick skillet under high heat, drizzle 1-2 tablespoons of olive oil. Toss in all the mushrooms and cook until the mushrooms have some caramelization (light browning). Add the fresh chopped herbs and set aside.

3. On a well floured surface begin to flatten the dough ball with your fingertips beginning from the inside out and moving in a circular fashion to create a thicker crust at the edges. You can now stretch the dough by dangling it from your fists or fingertips and moving in a circular fashion. This will take some practice. You can also try tossing the pizzas. Using your fists, again, cross your hands one over the other with the pizza dangling from your knuckles. With a quick tossing motion uncross your hands, in the process tossing the pizza into the air, spinning it and stretching it out in circular manner. Another option is to use a pin to roll out the pizzas. Pizza should be thin in the middle and thicker as you move out. Place the pizza on a floured peel (you can use a piece of cardboard if you don't have a peel).

4. Spread a thin layer of the sauce on the dough. Use as much sauce as you like. I don't like to use too much because it makes the pizza soggy after it has cooked. Spread a generous portion of the mushrooms. If you like you can add a light sprinkling of soy cheese. I do sometimes, but generally prefer to eat my pizzas without any cheese. Sprinkle some dried oregano.

5. Gently slide the pizza off the peel and onto the stone. If your peel is floured adequately, the pizza should slide right off. Bake until the bottom of the crust is a golden brown, 5-8 minutes. Place it under the broiler for a minute to brown the top of the crust.

*See Sauces and Dressings

Pizza Marinara

Servings: 4

INGREDIENTS:

1 recipe Pizza Dough (4 pizzas)
1 recipe Roasted Garlic Pizza Sauce*
fresh basil leaves
dried oregano
extra-virgin olive oil
soy cheese (non-dairy) optional

DIRECTIONS:

1. Once the dough has proofed (risen) for the second time and your oven with the baking stone is preheated to 450°F, you are ready to bake the pizzas.

2. On a well floured surface begin to flatten the dough ball with your fingertips beginning from the inside out and moving in a circular fashion to create a thicker crust at the edges. You can now stretch the dough by dangling it from your fists or fingertips and moving in a circular fashion. This will take some practice. You can also try tossing the pizzas. Using your fists, again, cross your hands one over the other with the pizza dangling from your knuckles. With a quick tossing motion uncross your hands, in the process tossing the pizza into the air, spinning it and stretching it out in circular manner. Another option is to use a pin to roll out the pizzas. Pizza should be thin in the middle and thicker as you move out. Place the pizza on a floured peel (you can use a piece of cardboard if you don't have a peel).

3. Lay out some fresh torn basil leaves onto the pizza. Spread a thin layer of the sauce on top of the basil. Use as much sauce as you like. I don't like to use too much because it makes the pizza soggy after it has cooked. If you like you can add a light sprinkling of soy cheese (it becomes Pizza Margherita with the added cheese). I do sometimes, but generally prefer to eat my pizzas without any cheese. Sprinkle some dried oregano and a very light drizzle of olive oil.

4. Gently slide the pizza off the peel and onto the stone. If your peel is floured adequately, the pizza should slide right off. Bake until the bottom of the crust is a golden brown, 5-8 minutes. Place it under the broiler for a minute to brown the top of the crust.

*See Sauces and Dressings

Pizza Portabella

Servings: 4

INGREDIENTS:

1 recipe Pizza Dough (4 pizzas)
1 recipe Roasted Garlic Pizza Sauce (See Sauces and Dressings)
6 Portabella Steaks
2 pounds fresh spinach
4 cloves fresh garlic, minced
fresh marjoram, thyme or oregano, chopped
dried oregano
extra-virgin olive oil

DIRECTIONS:

1. Once the dough has proofed (risen) for the second time and your oven with the baking stone is preheated to 450°F, you are ready to bake the pizzas.

2. Cook the portabella mushrooms before beginning this recipe. Throw in a handful of fresh chopped herbs before they are finished cooling. When they have cooled, slice them into bite-size wedges. You have to cook the spinach as well before using as a topping. You can either microwave or steam the spinach until it turns a bright green color. Drain off any excess water and chop the spinach well. Add the garlic to the spinach with a light drizzle of olive oil and sprinkle of salt.

3. On a well floured surface begin to flatten the dough ball with your fingertips beginning from the inside out and moving in a circular fashion to create a thicker crust at the edges. You can now stretch the dough by dangling it from your fists or fingertips and moving in a circular fashion. This will take some practice. You can also try tossing the pizzas. Using your fists, again, cross your hands one over the other with the pizza dangling from your knuckles. With a quick tossing motion uncross your hands, in the process tossing the pizza into the air, spinning it and stretching it out in circular manner. Another option is to use a pin to roll out the pizzas. Pizza should be thin in the middle and thicker as you move out. Place the pizza on a floured peel (you can use a piece of cardboard if you don't have a peel).

4. Spread a thin layer of the sauce on the dough. I don't like to use too much because it makes the pizza soggy after it has cooked. Spread a generous portion of the mushrooms. Place the spinach on the pizza in little clumps. Sprinkle some dried oregano and a light drizzle of olive oil if you like.

5. Gently slide the pizza off the peel and onto the stone. If your peel is floured adequately, the pizza should slide right off. Bake until the bottom of the crust is a golden brown, 5-8 minutes. Place it under the broiler for a minute to brown the top of the crust.

Banana Cranberry Nut Bread

INGREDIENTS:

2 cups whole wheat flour (pastry, if available)
1½ tsp. baking powder
½ tsp. baking soda
¼ tsp. salt
½ tsp. ground cinnamon
¼ tsp. ground nutmeg
1½ cups mashed banana (~ 5 medium)
1 1/8 cups light brown sugar
1 tsp. grated lemon (or orange) peel
Equivalent of 2 eggs using Egg Replacer™ (by ENER-G, instructions on box)
½ cup Firm Silken Tofu
¼ cup chopped walnuts, optional

DIRECTIONS:

1. Preheat oven to 350 °F.

2. In a mini food processor or a blender combine silken tofu, Egg Replacer powder and water required for Egg Replacer. Blend to smooth consistency.

3. Combine flour, baking powder, baking soda, salt, cinnamon and nutmeg in a separate bowl. Mix well, either with sifter or hand whisk.

4. Using a hand blender or Kitchen Aid (with batter blade), mash bananas. Add mixture from step 2, sugar and grated lemon peel. Blend well.

5. Lightly fold in mixture from step 3 until combined into banana mixture. Add walnuts and cranberries at this stage if desired.

6. Bake in a 9x5x3 inch pan, greased with non-stick baking spray, for 50-60 minutes or until toothpick comes out clean. Bread should be a golden brown color all around. Cool in pan for 10 minutes. Transfer to wire rack to finish cooling.

7. Bread freezes well. Use as French toast bread for a gourmet touch.

Braided Italian Bread

INGREDIENTS:

3½ cups unbleached all-purpose flour or bread flour
2/3 cup plus 1/2 cup lukewarm water
2 tsp. sugar
2 tsp. instant yeast
1¼ tsp. salt
unhulled toasted sesame seeds

DIRECTIONS (either by hand or using a Kitchen-Aid mixer):

1. Combine the water, yeast, sugar and salt until dissolved.

2. Add the flour and knead for about 7 minutes. Cover the dough and let rise for 1½ hours.

3. Transfer the dough to a non-floured surface and divide it into three equal pieces. Roll each piece into an 18-inch rope. Braid the ropes, tucking the ends under. Brush the dough lightly with water and sprinkle heavily with sesame seeds. Set aside on a baking sheet sprinkled with semolina or corn meal, and let rise another 1½ hours.

4. Bake at 450ºF for 30 minutes, preferably on a baking stone. Cool on a cooling rack.

5. I usually make double this recipe because it is not worth it to make just one loaf at a time. Besides, they disappear quickly.

Pancakes

INGREDIENTS:

Aunt Jemima Whole Wheat (or Regular) Pancake Mix
Soymilk (regular or vanilla, Edensoy™ brand, preferably)
fresh blueberries (optional)
fresh strawberries (optional)
dark chocolate chips (optional)

DIRECTIONS:

1. Preheat non-stick pan over medium-low heat.

2. Use as much pancake mix as you would like and add soymilk until the mixture attains the desired consistency. DO NOT add eggs or oil as the box calls for. These ingredients are not necessary, nor are they desirable.

3. Spray the pan with nonstick spray and immediately pour a ladle of the pancake batter. At this point you can add any ingredients you wish, such as blueberries or strawberries and occasionally it is OK to use dark chocolate.   Flip the pancake when the one side turns a golden brown and cook the other side until golden brown.

4. Enjoy with real maple syrup or maple butter (concentrated maple syrup, does not contain butter).

Spinach Pies

Servings: 6

INGREDIENTS:

1 recipe Pizza Dough (8 pizzas)
2 pounds fresh spinach, chiffonade
2 medium yellow onions, diced
3-4 fresh lemons, juiced
3 Tbs. extra-virgin olive oil
sumac
sea salt and cayenne pepper to taste

DIRECTIONS:

1. Prepare the dough as you would for making pizza, however, when you are ready to divide the dough into balls for the second rise or proofing, divide it into 12 balls (instead of 8 as the recipe calls for). Allow the dough to proof for the second time and preheat your oven with the baking stone to 450°F.

2. Chiffonade or julienne the spinach and add the remainder of the ingredients, including a generous sprinkling of sumac. On a well floured surface begin to flatten the dough balls with your fingertips going from the inside out and moving in a circular fashion. Unlike pizzas, you want the flattened dough to be the same thickness throughout. I use a rolling pin to do this, once I've used my fingertips to get it started. The flattened dough should be about 8-10 inches in diameter and less than 1/8 of an inch thick. Place two handfuls of the spinach salad into the middle of the pie, approximating a triangular shape. The pile should be heaping, but will cook down significantly during baking. The pie will be triangular when done. Turn over one edge of the dough onto the spinach filling. Then turn another side over. The two pieces of dough should meet at one corner. Turn over the third and final side onto the spinach and you have just created two additional corners. The sides of dough should overlap just a little, so you can close the pie (like a hamentash). Use your fingertips to seal the sides of dough together. Make all the pies this way.

3. Gently slide each spinach pie off the peel and onto the stone. If your peel is floured adequately, the pie should slide right off. Bake until the bottom of the crust is a golden brown, about 10 minutes. Place under the broiler for a minute to brown the top of the crust.

HINT: Save the juice from the filling and brush the pies when they come out of the oven. This will give it an extra kick and a nice sheen as well.

Sushi

Seasoned Rice Wine Vinegar (for Sushi)

INGREDIENTS:

2 parts rice wine vinegar
1 part sugar
1/4 part salt

DIRECTIONS:

Recipes for dressings work better in proportions so that you can make as much as you want. For example, if you wanted to make ½ cup of seasoned rice wine vinegar (which is what the sushi recipe calls for), you would use: 8 Tbs. vinegar, 4 Tbs. sugar, and ¼ Tbs. salt. You will need to heat the mixture slightly to dissolve all of the sugar.

Sushi Rice

INGREDIENTS:

3 cups uncooked short grain rice
1/2 cup seasoned rice wine vinegar

DIRECTIONS:

Do not wash white rice. Vitamins taken away in the processing of white rice are added back in powder form. If you wash the rice, you wash away valuable nutrients. Cook the rice, preferably in a rice cooker. You can make the rice in a pot (for 3 cups rice use 3 1/3 cups water). Traditionally the seasoned rice wine vinegar is added in slowly, while the rice is being fanned. This, of course, may not be practical. I mix it in under an electric fan. Fanning the rice as you add the vinegar gives the rice a nicer texture and gloss. Though, it really is not necessary to cool the rice while adding the vinegar. Cool the rice until it is lukewarm to touch. You do not want the rice to be cold as it will become hard. Also, you can buy seasoned rice wine vinegar anywhere unseasoned rice wine vinegar is sold, but if you want to make it yourself, follow the recipe at the beginning of this section. Once the seasoned vinegar is added, the rice is ready to be used for sushi or just to eat plain. You can cover the rice with a wet towel or plastic wrap to keep it from drying out.

Brown Sushi Rice

INGREDIENTS:

3 cups uncooked short grain brown rice
1/2 cup seasoned rice wine vinegar

DIRECTIONS:

Brown rice is a healthier alternative to white rice, though, it is not as sticky as white rice and is not the traditional rice of sushi. Cook the rice, preferably in a rice cooker. You can make the rice in a pot (for 3 cups rice use 4 1/2 cups water). Traditionally the seasoned rice wine vinegar is added in slowly, while the rice is being fanned. This, of course, is not practical. I mix it in under an electric fan. Fanning the rice as you add the vinegar gives the rice a nicer texture and gloss. Though, it really is not necessary to cool the rice while adding the vinegar. Cool the rice until it is lukewarm to touch. You do not want the rice to be cold as it will become hard. Also, you can buy seasoned rice wine vinegar anywhere unseasoned rice wine vinegar is sold, but if you want to make it yourself, follow the recipe at the beginning of this section. Once the seasoned vinegar is added, the rice is ready to be used for sushi or just to eat plain. You can cover the rice with a wet towel or put it back into the rice cooker to keep it warm.

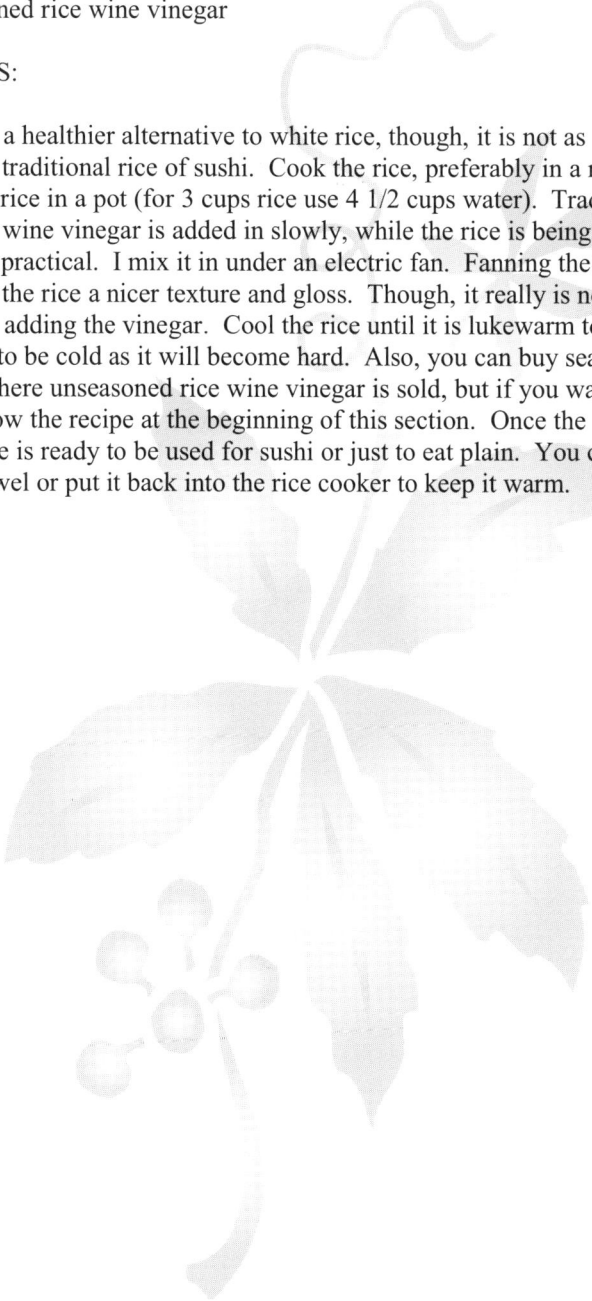

Basic Vegetarian Sushi

Servings: 2-3

INGREDIENTS:

6 sheets nori (toasted seaweed)
1 recipe Sushi or Brown Sushi Rice
1 English cucumber
1 large carrot
soy sauce
toasted unhulled sesame seeds
wasabi powder or paste (Japanese horseradish)
hot sauce (Sriracha™)
pickled ginger

EQUIPMENT:

sushi or bamboo mat (for rolling sushi)
bowl cold water

DIRECTIONS:

1. Before you do anything, start cooking the rice.

2. Vegetables must be cut just right if you want sushi to look nice once you are done. The goal is to cut long, thin, even strips of vegetables that are either the width or half the width of a sheet of nori. This holds true for carrots and cucumber, but not for avocado. For avocado, you want to cut roughly rectangular pieces, so you use as much of it as possible. I cut it along its natural shape and overlap the slices when I roll the sushi. That way, I don't waste anything.

3. Once your vegetables are prepped and your sushi rice is prepared according to the recipe, you are ready to roll. The goal is to roll tight, even rolls of sushi. This will produce the best results once you cut the rolls. Begin by laying out a sheet of nori on the bamboo mat, shiny side facing down. With your hands dipped in cold water, take a clump of the sushi rice and begin to spread it onto the nori. The best way is to take little clumps at a time and use your fingertips to spread. I like to have a thin of layer of rice, about ½ cm, so I can fit more vegetables in the roll. Dip your fingers into the water if they get too sticky (be sure to keep any water away from the nori because it will ruin it). You do not want to spread the rice to all the edges. The nori sheet is cut into sections and you will find that the two sections at the edge nearest to and farthest from you are considerably smaller than the other sections. You want to stay within these sections so you can seal your roll. Be sure to spread the rice all the way to the side edges, however.

4. You will be placing the filling on the side closest to you. First, sprinkle sesame seeds lightly over the rice. On the edge of the rice, of the side closest to you, lay down your vegetables. I like to use a filling that is at least twice as thick and high as the thickness of rice on the sheet. Using the bamboo mat, grab the edge closest to you (the part without rice on it) and fold the nori over the filling to cover the filling completely. Using your fingers, tightly grip the sushi mat over the roll, pulling towards yourself. Do this for the entire width of the roll. Turn the mat another 90° (quarter turn of roll) away from you and grip the roll with your fingertips again, tucking the roll as tight as you can and pulling towards yourself. Do this a few more times and your roll is done. Be sure to hold the roll down for a little bit longer on the last roll so your roll seals well. You should have a tight, compact roll that is square in appearance.

5. Slice each roll into 8-12 pieces using a sharp chef's knife or a serrated knife. For this recipe you can make 2 rolls each of cucumber, carrot and avocado. You can make any combination you like.

6. For dipping, use soy sauce with a tiny bit of wasabi paste mixed in. I like to add a bit of Sriracha hot sauce instead. Wasabi clears out my sinuses far too well. Pickled ginger goes well with every bite.

California Roll Sushi

Servings: 2-3

INGREDIENTS:

6 sheets nori (toasted seaweed)
1 recipe Sushi or Brown Sushi Rice
1 recipe Pan-Fried Tofu*
1 avocado
1 English cucumber
plum paste (umeboshi)
fresh Thai basil, julienned
toasted unhulled sesame seeds
soy sauce
wasabi powder or paste (Japanese horseradish)
hot sauce (Sriracha™)
pickled ginger

EQUIPMENT:

sushi or bamboo mat (for rolling sushi)
bowl cold water

DIRECTIONS:

1. Before you do anything, start cooking the rice.

2. As with vegetables, tofu must be cut just right if you want sushi to look nice once you are done. The goal is to cut long, thin, even strips of tofu once it has been cooked. What you want to do is cut the block of tofu into about 8 pieces, cook it according to the recipe and cut into thin strips once it has cooled.

3. Once the tofu and the other vegetables are prepped and your sushi rice is prepared according to the recipe, you are ready to roll. California roll has no definitive recipe. Everyone has their own version. The common theme seems to be avocado in almost every recipe I've seen. This happens to be my version of a California roll. For directions on rolling, see Basic Vegetarian Sushi. For this roll, you want to lay down a very thin strip of the plum paste before you lay down your vegetables. Put equal amounts of tofu, cucumber and avocado into the roll. Finally, add some strips of julienned Thai basil. Roll this sushi as you would any other. You can also do an inverted roll with the rice on the outside. I suggest you only try this if you feel comfortable with the traditional roll.

*See Appetizers and Side Dishes

Portabella Sushi

Servings: 2-3

INGREDIENTS:

6 sheets nori (toasted seaweed)
1 recipe Sushi or Brown Sushi Rice
3 Portabella Steaks*
toasted unhulled sesame seeds
soy sauce
wasabi powder or paste (Japanese horseradish)
hot sauce (Sriracha™)
pickled ginger

EQUIPMENT:

sushi or bamboo mat (for rolling sushi)
bowl cold water

DIRECTIONS:

1. Before you do anything, start cooking the rice.

2. Cook the portabella steaks as the recipe specifies; however, substitute 2/3 cup Garlic Sauce** for the marinade. When the mushroom caps have cooled, slice into long thin strips.

3. When the mushrooms are done and your sushi rice is prepared according to the recipe, you are ready to roll. For directions on rolling, see Basic Vegetarian Sushi.

*See Appetizers and Side Dishes

**See Sauces and Dressings

Red Pepper Basil Sushi

Servings: 2-3

INGREDIENTS:

6 sheets nori (toasted seaweed)
1 recipe Sushi or Brown Sushi Rice
2 sweet red peppers, very thinly sliced
1 small yellow onion, very thinly sliced
3 cloves fresh minced garlic
1 tsp. fresh grated ginger
handful Thai or regular basil, julienned
1 tsp. sesame oil
1 tsp. extra-virgin olive oil
toasted unhulled sesame seeds
soy sauce
wasabi powder or paste (Japanese horseradish)
hot sauce (Sriracha™)
pickled ginger

EQUIPMENT:

sushi or bamboo mat (for rolling sushi)
bowl cold water

DIRECTIONS:

1. Before you do anything, start cooking the rice.

2. In a hot sauté pan, add sesame and olive oils, red pepper and onion. Cook until the onions start to brown. Add garlic and ginger. Cook until garlic starts to brown. Deglaze the vegetables with a splash of soy sauce. When all the liquid has evaporated, turn heat off and mix in basil.

3. Once the vegetables are done and your sushi rice is prepared according to the recipe, you are ready to roll. For directions on rolling, see Basic Vegetarian Sushi.

Cooked Squash Sushi

Servings: 2-3

INGREDIENTS:

6 sheets nori (toasted seaweed)
1 recipe Sushi or Brown Sushi Rice
3 medium size zucchini, thinly julienned
3 cloves fresh minced garlic
1 tsp. fresh grated ginger
1 tsp. extra-virgin olive oil
toasted unhulled sesame seeds
soy sauce
wasabi powder or paste (Japanese horseradish)
hot sauce (Sriracha™)
pickled ginger

EQUIPMENT:

sushi or bamboo mat (for rolling sushi)
bowl cold water

DIRECTIONS:

1. Before you do anything, start cooking the rice.

2. In a hot sauté pan, add olive oil and julienned zucchini. Cook until the zucchini is wilted and begins to brown. Add garlic and ginger. Cook until garlic starts to brown. Deglaze the squash with a splash of soy sauce. When all the liquid has evaporated, turn heat off.

3. Once the squash is cooked and your sushi rice prepared according to the recipe, you are ready to roll. For directions on rolling, see Basic Vegetarian Sushi.

Tofu Sushi

Servings: 2-3

INGREDIENTS:

6 sheets nori (toasted seaweed)
1 recipe Sushi or Brown Sushi Rice
1 recipe Pan-Fried Tofu*
toasted unhulled sesame seeds
soy sauce
wasabi powder or paste (Japanese horseradish)
hot sauce (Sriracha™)
pickled ginger

EQUIPMENT:

sushi or bamboo mat (for rolling sushi)
bowl cold water

DIRECTIONS:

1. Before you do anything, start cooking the rice.

2. As with vegetables, tofu must be cut just right if you want sushi to look nice once you are done. The goal is to cut long, thin, even strips of tofu once it has been cooked. What you want to do is cut the block of tofu into about 8 pieces, cook it according to the recipe and cut into thin strips once it has cooled.

3. Once the tofu is prepped and your sushi rice is prepared according to the recipe, you are ready to roll. For directions on rolling, see Basic Vegetarian Sushi.

*See Appetizers and Side Dishes

Entrees

Broccoli Stir Fry

Servings: 4

INGREDIENTS:

2 pounds broccoli
½ pound snow peas
4 carrots
½ pound cooked Tofu, Grilled, Baked or Pan-fried*
4 cloves fresh minced garlic
1 tsp. fresh grated ginger
2 tsp. sesame oil
water
½-2/3 cup Spicy Garlic Sauce**
corn starch
rice, any variety

DIRECTIONS:

1. Start cooking enough rice for four people before preparing anything else. Cut the broccoli into large bite size pieces. Leave the snow peas whole. Slice the carrots on a diagonal. You want to blanch or steam these veggies until the broccoli is a bright green color. To blanch, place the veggies into a pot of boiling, salted water. Blanch the carrots with the broccoli. When the broccoli turns a bright green, both the carrots and broccoli are done. Do the same with the snow peas. Meanwhile you should have your wok or large frying pan heating up over a high flame.

2. Dissolve about 1 ½ tsp. corn starch in 2 Tbs. water. Add this slurry to the garlic sauce. Stir well and make sure there are no clumps. Set aside.

3. In the hot wok, cook the garlic and ginger in the sesame oil. These will cook in less than 30 seconds. Quickly add all the vegetables and tofu. Stir until they are all mixed. Add the garlic sauce/corn starch slurry mixture. Do not stir. Allow a few seconds for the sauce to come to a boil and for the sauce to change from cloudy to clear. At this point stir the vegetables into the sauce. The sauce will be very thick at this point. Add the sesame seeds and stir again. Arrange the vegetables on a plate.

*See Appetizers and Side Dishes

** See Sauces and Dressings

Chinese Broccoli in Garlic Sauce

Servings: 4

INGREDIENTS:

2 1/2 -3 pounds Chinese broccoli
4 cloves fresh minced garlic
1 tsp. grated ginger
2 tsp. sesame oil
½-2/3 cup Spicy Garlic Sauce*
corn starch
water
rice, any variety

DIRECTIONS:

1. Start cooking enough rice for four people before preparing anything else.

2. Chinese broccoli is a little known or appreciated vegetable outside of Chinese cuisine. In my opinion, it is an exquisite vegetable. I owe my knowledge of this vegetable to my friend, Andy, who first introduced me to it in college. Chinese broccoli is just a type of broccoli that is mostly stem. It has a nuttier flavor than regular broccoli and is just a pleasure to the palate. Cut the broccoli stems into halves or thirds depending on how large they are. You want to blanch or steam these veggies until they are a bright green color. To blanch, place the veggies into a pot of boiling, salted water. When the broccoli turns a bright green, it's done. Meanwhile you should have your wok or large frying pan heating up over a high flame.

3. Dissolve about 1 ½ tsp. corn starch in 2 Tbs. water. Add this slurry to the garlic sauce. Stir well and make sure there are no clumps. Set aside.

4. In the hot wok, cook the garlic and ginger in the sesame oil. These will cook in less than 30 seconds. Quickly add the broccoli. Stir until the ingredients are well mixed. Add the garlic sauce/corn starch slurry mixture. Do not stir. Allow a few seconds for the sauce to come to a boil and for the sauce to change from cloudy to clear. At this point stir the broccoli into the sauce. The sauce will be very thick, so act quickly. Serve the broccoli with a side of rice.

*See Sauces and Dressings

Gingered Zucchini Nut Curry

Servings: 4

INGREDIENTS:

2 seeded hot green chilies (or as desired)
1-inch piece of fresh ginger root, scraped and roughly chopped
3 Tbs. almonds
1½ Tbs. coriander seeds
1 tsp. cumin seeds
¼ tsp. fennel seeds
¼ - ½ cup water
3 Tbs. extra-virgin olive oil
2 medium-sized tomatoes, peeled, seeded and chopped
1½ pounds zucchini, peeled and cut into ½ -inch cubes
½ tsp. turmeric
1 tsp. salt
handful of chopped fresh coriander

DIRECTIONS:

1. Combine green chilies, ginger root, almonds, coriander seeds, cumin seeds, fennel seeds and water in a blender. Cover and process until smooth paste.

2. Heat the oil in a large heavy nonstick saucepan over medium heat. Pour in the spice puree and cook until it thickens and just begins to brown. Stir in the tomatoes and cook for a few minutes. Add the squash, turmeric, salt and half of the fresh coriander, stir, cover and cook over low heat for about 10 minutes. Occasionally stir and scrape the squash from the bottom of the pan to prevent sticking. If the squash is dry, add a little water. Cook until the squash is soft and all the excess water has cooked off (about 30 minutes). Before serving, sprinkle with the remaining fresh coriander.

Green Beans with Tomatoes

Servings: 4

INGREDIENTS:

2 pounds fresh green beans (preferably, Italian flat beans or Chinese string beans)
4 large tomatoes, diced
1 whole head of garlic, peeled
1 large yellow onion
2 Tbs. extra-virgin olive oil
crushed red pepper flakes to taste
sea salt to taste

1 recipe, Rice Pilaf*
fresh pita

DIRECTIONS:

Wash the string beans and snap into large bite size pieces. In a large pot, add oil, onions and whole garlic cloves. Sauté until onions and garlic are lightly browned. Add green beans and a sprinkle of salt. Cover and cook over medium heat, stirring occasionally. When the green beans are wilted and browned (about 20 minutes), add the tomatoes. Cook, uncovered, for an additional 15 minutes or so, until tomatoes have broken down and most of the liquid is gone. Season with salt and pepper. Enjoy warm or cold, with rice pilaf or fresh hot pita.

*See Appetizers and Side Dishes

Leek-Dill Bulgur

Servings: 4

INGREDIENTS:

3 medium-sized leeks
1 bunch dill
½ cup coarse whole wheat bulgur
1 ½ cups cold water
2 Tbs. extra-virgin olive oil
½ tsp. salt to taste
crushed red pepper to taste

DIRECTIONS:

1. Julienne leeks and wash thoroughly (at least three times). Set aside. Finely chop dill and set aside.

2. In a sauce pan over medium heat sauté leeks with salt in olive oil until just wilted. Add the dill and bulgur. Fry together for a few minutes, than add water all at once. Bring the mixture to a boil, turn heat to low and cover pan. Stir occasionally to prevent it from sticking. If necessary add additional water until bulgur wheat is completely cooked. Bulgur is completely cooked when the grain "pops" open. It will approximately triple in size by the time it is fully cooked.

3. Enjoy with crushed red pepper or your favorite hot sauce.

Lentils with Rice

Servings: 6

INGREDIENTS:

2 cups dry lentils
2 medium yellow onions, diced
3 Tbs. extra-virgin olive oil
1 cup long grain rice
sea salt to taste

DIRECTIONS:

1. In at least a 4 quart pot, add lentils and water to cover by one inch. Bring this mixture
to a boil and cook until the lentils are tender. Meanwhile you can prepare the onions.

2. In a skillet, sauté onions in olive oil until well caramelized (uniform brown hue).
When lentils are done cooking, turn heat down to simmer, add the cooked onions, one
cup of rice and salt. If necessary, add water to cover by ½ inch. Cover and simmer on
very low heat until the rice is cooked and no liquid remains. Enjoy with pickled turnips,
wild cucumbers and your favorite salad.

VARIATION:

For an even more nutritious meal, use coarse whole wheat bulgur instead of rice and cook
the same way.

Linguine with Broccoli Rabe

Servings: 4

INGREDIENTS:

2 pounds broccoli rabe
1-1 ½ cups Marinara Sauce*
2 Tbs. extra-virgin olive oil
10 cloves fresh garlic, thinly sliced
½ tsp. crushed red pepper flakes
sea salt to taste

1 pound dried linguine

DIRECTIONS:

1. Begin boiling water before you start prepping. When water boils add pasta and cook until al-dente. When you bite into the pasta it still bites back just a little bit. While the water is boiling you can prepare the broccoli rabe.

2. Wash the broccoli rabe and cut each stem into thirds. Set aside. Meanwhile, five minutes before the pasta is done, in a hot skillet or sauté pan, add oil, chili flakes and garlic. Cook until garlic just starts to brown. Add the broccoli rabe and cook until it turns a bright green color. Add enough marinara sauce (you can run the marina sauce through the food mill or food processor so there are no large pieces of onion or tomato) to give the dish some added color, but not so much that the broccoli is drowning in sauce. When the sauce comes up to temperature, turn off the burner. Taste and add salt if needed.   Serve the broccoli over the linguine in a large bowl or on individual plates.

*See Sauces and Dressings

Mushroom Farfalle (Bowties)

Servings: 4

INGREDIENTS:

6 Portabella Steaks*
1 cup sun-dried tomatoes
2 Tbs. extra-virgin olive oil
8 cloves fresh garlic, crushed
sea salt and crushed red pepper to taste
handful fresh basil, julienned

1 pound dried farfalle (bowtie pasta)

DIRECTIONS:

1. Cook the portabella mushrooms before beginning this recipe. When they have cooled, slice them into bite-size wedges. Begin boiling salted water before you start prepping the remainder of the ingredients. When the water boils add pasta and cook until al-dente. When you bite into the pasta it still bites back just a little bit.

2. I recommend using sun-dried tomatoes that are not in oil. The extra oil is not at all necessary. Good quality sun-dried tomatoes are not completely dry either. They have some moisture to them and should be edible without pre-soaking. Slice the tomatoes into thin strips. If they are very dry, soak in warm water for ½ hour first. Julienne the tomatoes.

3. Meanwhile, a few minutes before the pasta is done, in a hot skillet or sauté pan, add oil and garlic. Cook until garlic just starts to brown. Add the mushrooms and sun-dried tomatoes. Add the pasta and basil. Toss, season with salt and pepper and serve in a large bowl or individual plates.

*See Appetizers and Side Dishes

Pasta Primavera

Servings: 4

INGREDIENTS:

1 pound broccoli
1 sweet red pepper, sliced
1 pound crimini mushrooms sliced
1 cup sun-dried tomatoes
2-3 Tbs. extra-virgin olive oil
10 cloves fresh garlic, thinly sliced
1 handful basil, julienned
1 handful marjoram, roughly chopped
¾ cup white wine
1-1½ cups Marinara Sauce* (optional)
½ tsp. crushed red pepper flakes
sea salt to taste

1 pound dried ziti

DIRECTIONS:

1. Begin boiling salted water for the pasta before you start prepping. When water boils add pasta and cook until al-dente. When you bite into the pasta it still bites back just a little bit.

2. Cut the broccoli into bite-size pieces and set aside. I recommend using sun-dried tomatoes that are not in oil. The extra oil is not at all necessary. Good quality sun-dried tomatoes are not completely dry either. They have some moisture to them and should be edible without pre-soaking. Slice the tomatoes into thin strips. If they are very dry, soak in warm water for ½ hour first.

3. In a hot skillet or sauté pan, add oil, mushrooms and peppers. Sauté until mushrooms are browned. Add chili flakes and garlic. Cook until garlic just starts to brown. Add the broccoli, sun-dried tomatoes and white wine. Cook until broccoli turns a bright green color. Add basil and marjoram. Toss.

4. I like to toss in the pasta as well, but you can just serve the vegetables over the pasta. If you are in the mood for a red sauce you can toss in a cup or so of marinara sauce or add it to each individual plate over the veggies.

*See Sauces and Dressings

Penne Arrabiata

Servings: 4

INGREDIENTS:

½ recipe of Marinara Sauce*
2 Tbs. extra-virgin olive oil
6 cloves fresh garlic, crushed
1 tsp. crushed red pepper flakes
handful fresh basil, julienned

1 pound dried penne pasta

DIRECTIONS:

Begin boiling salted water for the pasta before you start prepping. When water boils add pasta and cook until al-dente. When you bite into the pasta it still bites back just a little bit. Meanwhile, a few minutes before the pasta is done, in a hot skillet or sauté pan, add oil, chili flakes and garlic. Cook until garlic just starts to brown. Add the basil and cook for a few seconds. Add marinara sauce (you can run the marina sauce through the food mill or food processor so there are no pieces of onion or tomato). Add the cooked pasta to the mixture. Alternatively, you could add the sauce and then serve in a large bowl or individual plates over cooked pasta.

*See Sauces and Dressings

Pignoli Eggplant

Servings: 4

INGREDIENTS:

3 large eggplant, peeled and cut into ¾ inch pieces
4 medium sized tomatoes, diced
1 medium sized onion, chopped
8 cloves garlic, thinly sliced
2 Tbs. extra-virgin olive oil
2 Tbs. pignoli or pine nuts
sea salt and crushed red pepper to taste

DIRECTIONS:

In a large stew pot over medium heat, sauté chopped onion in olive oil until translucent. Add the garlic and cook until garlic just starts to brown. Add the eggplant, tomato and a sprinkle of salt all at once, stir and cover. When mixture begins to boil, turn heat to low. Cook until the eggplant is mushy and the tomatoes have broken down, about 30-40 minutes. If there is a lot of liquid in the pot, uncover and cook until liquid has evaporated. In a hot dry skillet toast pignoli until they are golden brown. Sprinkle on top of the eggplant when served. Enjoy with Rice Pilaf* or warm pita.

*See Appetizers and Side Dishes

Ratatouille

Servings: 4

INGREDIENTS:

2 large eggplant, peeled and cut into ¾ inch pieces
4 yellow squash and/or zucchini, cut into ¾ inch pieces
3 medium sized tomatoes, diced
1 medium sized onion, chopped
2 hot green chilies, any variety seeded and julienned
2 Tbs. extra-virgin olive oil
salt to taste

DIRECTIONS:

In a large stew pot over medium heat, sauté chopped onion in olive oil until translucent. Add the remainder of the vegetables and a sprinkle of salt all at once, stir and cover. When mixture begins to boil, turn heat to low. Cook until the eggplant is very soft and the tomatoes have broken down, about 30 minutes. Enjoy warm or cold with pita bread.

Savory Baby Peas

INGREDIENTS:

1 pound baby peas fresh or frozen
1 medium sized onion, chopped
1 can tomato paste (6 oz.)
1 cup water or red wine
2 Tbs. extra-virgin olive oil
¾ tsp. salt to taste

DIRECTIONS:

Sauté chopped onion in olive oil until translucent and just beginning to brown. Then add peas all at once and sauté for 5 minutes. Add tomato paste and cook for two minutes. Add water or wine, cover partially and simmer for 20 minutes. Add salt at the end.

Optional: Add your favorite variety of mushroom and sauté for 10 minutes or until browned before adding the peas.

Spinach Tofu Lasagna

Servings: 6-8

INGREDIENTS:

2 pounds (blocks) firm or extra-firm tofu
2 pounds fresh spinach
1 ½ - 2 pounds crimini mushrooms, sliced
1 handful sun-dried tomatoes
4 Tbs. extra-virgin olive oil and additional for topping
handful fresh basil, marjoram and or thyme
8 cloves fresh garlic, peeled
sea salt and crushed red pepper to taste
plain bread crumbs
1 clove fresh garlic, crushed
1 bunch fresh Italian parsley, minced
soy mozzarella cheese, dairy-free (optional)

2 recipes, Marinara Sauce (See Sauces and Dressings)
1 pound dried lasagna noodles

DIRECTIONS:

1. Begin boiling salted water before you start prepping the remainder of the ingredients. When the water boils add the lasagna and cook half way through (it will cook completely in the oven). Put the cooked lasagna into a large bowl of ice water to stop cooking.

2. In a food processor, purée the tofu and garlic to a smooth consistency. Add the sun-dried tomatoes, 2 Tbs. olive oil, fresh herbs, salt and pepper. Combine until tomatoes are chopped into fine pieces.

3. In a hot skillet or sauté pan, add 2 Tbs. olive oil and all the mushrooms. Cook until mushrooms are well browned. Steam or microwave the spinach to a bright green color. Drain off any excess fluid and julienne.

4. Now you're ready to assemble the lasagna. Preheat the oven to 375°F. In a 9x13 inch deep baking dish, put a layer of marinara sauce, then a layer of pasta (patted dry), then a layer of the tofu mixture, some mushrooms, some spinach, another layer of sauce, another layer of pasta and so on until you have used up everything (you may have leftover sauce). For the top layer, put pasta, then sauce. Finally, sprinkle on some bread crumbs mixed with fresh parsley, fresh crushed garlic, olive oil and salt (if you like, you can also sprinkle on some grated soy cheese). Cover with foil and bake until pasta is thoroughly cooked through and very little liquid remains, about 45 minutes. Uncover to brown the top for the last 10 minutes.

Stewed Okra

INGREDIENTS:

2 pounds fresh okra (small and tender)
4 large tomatoes or 1 can plum tomatoes, diced
1 jalapeno, deseeded and deveined, julienned
5 cloves fresh garlic, thinly sliced
2 Tbs. extra-virgin olive oil
sea salt to taste

1 recipe Rice Pilaf*

DIRECTIONS:

Wash the okra and cut off the stems. Leave the okra whole. In a large sauce pan, add oil and whole garlic cloves. Sauté until garlic is lightly browned. Add okra, jalapeno, and a sprinkle of salt. Cover and cook over medium heat, stirring occasionally. When the okra is wilted and browned (about 20 minutes), add the tomatoes. Cover and cook for an additional 20 minutes or so, until tomatoes have broken down. Season with salt and pepper. Enjoy warm or cold, with rice pilaf or fresh, hot pita.

HINT: If you find okra slimy, you can do the following. In a 300°F oven, bake the okra on sheet pans until they are very lightly browned and have a dry consistency. Use as you would in the above recipe. Traditionally, okra was deep-fried before using in recipes. This is an unnecessary step that adds time and fat.

*See Appetizers and Side Dishes

Truffle and Thyme Linguine

INGREDIENTS:

1 Truffle, any variety, at least ½ ounce, very thinly sliced

(Truffle is a delicate wild mushroom harvested from beneath oak trees. They can range in price from $80/lb. to $1500/lb. The best truffles are imported from France and Italy, but they are cultivated domestically as well.)

8 cloves garlic, thinly sliced
1 bunch fresh thyme, finely chopped
2 Tbs. extra-virgin olive oil
salt and crushed red pepper to taste
white wine (optional)

1 pound dried linguine

DIRECTIONS:

Begin to cook the pasta before you begin prepping the ingredients. The pasta will finish cooking before your dish is done, but since you will cook it al-dente, you don't have to worry about overcooking your pasta. In a hot pan over low heat, sauté the garlic in the olive oil until it begins to brown. Add the truffle slices. Cook for only about 30 seconds, and then quickly add the pasta, tossing all the ingredients together. Add the thyme, salt and red pepper flakes to taste. You may want to add a touch of white wine or water if the pasta is too sticky. The dish is done. Enjoy immediately. This is not a dish for everyday. If you really want to enjoy the fine culinary rarities of this world, however, you can not go without trying truffles at least once. This is a simple, but truly amazing dish!

Vegetable Lo Mein

Servings: 4-6

INGREDIENTS:

1 pound broccoli
½ pound snow peas
2 carrots
½ pound cooked tofu, Grilled, Baked or Pan-fried (See Appetizers and Side Dishes)
10 ounces fresh mushrooms, sliced
1 sweet red pepper, thinly sliced
½ cup water chestnuts
1 cup Chinese or Napa cabbage, julienned
4 cloves fresh minced garlic
1 tsp. grated ginger
1 Tbs. sesame oil

1 pound egg-free lo mein noodles or thin linguine
1/2-2/3 cup Spicy Garlic Sauce (See Sauces and Dressings)
corn starch
water

DIRECTIONS:

1. Start boiling salted water for the noodles. Cook the noodles al-dente, so they bite back at you a little. Cut the broccoli into large bite size pieces. Leave the snow peas whole. Slice the carrots on a diagonal. You want to blanch or steam these veggies until they are a bright green color. To blanch, place the veggies into a pot of boiling, salted water. Blanch the carrots with the broccoli. When the broccoli turns a bright green, both the carrots and broccoli are done. Do the same with the snow peas. Meanwhile you should have your wok or large frying pan heating up over a high flame.

2. Dissolve about 1 ½ tsp. corn starch in 2 Tbs. water. Add this slurry to the garlic sauce. Stir well and make sure there are no clumps. Set aside.

3. In the hot wok, add the oil, peppers and mushrooms. Cook these for about five minutes. Add the garlic and ginger. These will cook in about 1-2 minutes. Add the remaining vegetables and tofu. Stir until they are all mixed. Throw in the noodles, and add the garlic sauce/corn starch slurry mixture. Do not sir. Allow a few seconds for the sauce to come to a boil and for the sauce to change from cloudy to clear. At this point add the cabbage and stir everything into the sauce. The sauce will be very thick, so act quickly. Sir fry until all the ingredients are well combined and there is almost no liquid remaining. The dish is ready to enjoy.

Vermicelli Stir Fry

INGREDIENTS:

1 ½ pounds broccoli
½ pound snow peas
1 pound cooked Tofu, Grilled, Baked or Pan-fried*
1 pound fresh crimini and/or shitake mushrooms, sliced
1 sweet red pepper, thinly sliced
2 cups Chinese or Napa cabbage, julienned
4 cloves fresh minced garlic
1 tsp. grated ginger
1 Tbs. sesame oil
1 Tbs. extra-virgin olive oil

1 pound vermicelli rice noodles
1/2-2/3 cup Spicy Garlic Sauce**

DIRECTIONS:

1. Start heating water for the noodles. Cook the noodles according to package directions. This usually means soaking the noodles in hot water until they are cooked. When the noodles are done, drain and add ½ Tbs. olive oil and work through to coat all noodles. Cut the broccoli into large bite size pieces. Chiffonade the snow peas into 3 or 4 pieces each. You want to blanch or steam these veggies until they are a bright green color. To blanch, place the veggies into a pot of boiling, salted water. When the broccoli turns a bright green, it is done. Do the same with the snow peas. Meanwhile you should have your wok or large frying pan heating up over a high flame.

2. In the hot wok, add the sesame and remaining olive oils, peppers and mushrooms. Cook these for about five minutes or until the mushrooms are lightly browned. Add the garlic and ginger. These will cook in about 1-2 minutes. Add the remaining vegetables (except cabbage) and tofu. Stir until they are all mixed. Throw in the noodles, and add the garlic sauce, tossing as you combine the sauce. At this point add the cabbage and continue to toss. Sir fry until all the ingredients are well combined.

*See Appetizers and Side Dishes

**See Sauces and Dressings

Desserts

Apple Crisp

INGREDIENTS:

Crumb Topping:

1 cup almonds, whole
2/3 cup silken tofu
4 Tbs. Amaretto Liqueur
1 ¾ cups light brown sugar
1 ¾ cups whole wheat or unbleached white flour
1 ¾ cups whole grain oats
1 tsp. cinnamon
½ tsp. nutmeg
¼ tsp. salt

Apple Filling:

10-12 large baking apples (Granny Smith), peeled and sliced (equivalent to 10 cups sliced apples)
1½ tsp. cinnamon
1 cup light brown sugar
2 Tbs. corn starch

DIRECTIONS:

1. Preheat oven to 375 °F.

2. In a food processor grind almonds to fine consistency, then add tofu and Amaretto Liqueur. Puree to a smooth texture.

3. In a large bowl combine flour, 1 ¾ cups light brown sugar, oats, salt, cinnamon and nutmeg. Use a whisk to obtain a homogenous mixture. To this mixture add the mixture from step 2. Incorporate using a fork until you have a moist crumbly texture.

4. In a separate bowl combine sliced apples, cinnamon, light brown sugar and corn starch.

5. Spread apple mixture in 9x13 inch glass or ceramic pan. Crumble topping over apples. Cover with aluminum foil and bake for ½ hour. Uncover and bake another 15 minutes.

Optional: Enjoy with a low-fat dairy-free frozen vanilla dessert.

Apple Pie

INGREDIENTS:

1 recipe Whole Wheat Pastry Dough*
8 tart (Granny Smith or Fuji) apples, peeled and thinly sliced
1 cup light brown sugar
2 Tbs. corn starch
1 tsp. ground cinnamon
¼ tsp. nutmeg
¼ tsp. sea salt
soy milk and coarse granulated sugar (optional)

DIRECTIONS:

Preheat oven to 400°F. Roll out the pastry dough to make the top and bottom of a 9 inch pie. Combine all the ingredients. Lay down the bottom crust in a 9 inch pie pan. Pour the filling into the pie. Lay down the top crust. Crimp and flute the edges. Make one or two decorative slits in the top crust to allow steam to escape. You can brush the top with soy milk and sprinkle on some coarse granulated sugar. Bake in the lower 1/3 of the oven for about 50 minutes or until pie crust is golden brown and filling is bubbling.

HINT: Wrap the edge of the pie with aluminum foil to prevent it from burning. Uncover for the last ten minutes of baking. Bake the pie on a sheet pan to catch any drippings.

*At end of this section

Blueberry Pie

INGREDIENTS:

1 recipe Whole Wheat Pastry Dough*
6 cups fresh blueberries
1 cup light brown sugar
2 Tbs. corn starch
2 Tbs. unbleached flour
½ tsp. ground cinnamon
¼ tsp. sea salt
grated rind of 1 lemon
confectioner's sugar (optional)

DIRECTIONS:

Preheat oven to 400°F. Roll out the pastry dough to make the top and bottom of a 9 inch pie. Combine all the ingredients. Lay down the bottom crust in a 9 inch pie pan. Pour the filling into the pie. Lay down the top crust. Crimp and flute the edges. Make one or two decorative slits in the top crust to allow steam to escape. Bake in the lower 1/3 of the oven for about 50 minutes or until pie crust is golden brown and filling is bubbling. Allow to cool before sprinkling the top with powdered sugar.

HINT: Wrap the edge of the pie with aluminum foil to prevent it from burning. Uncover for the last ten minutes of baking. Bake the pie on sheet pan to catch any drippings.

*At end of this section

Low-fat Brownies

INGREDIENTS:

1 package of your favorite brownie mix
1 equivalent of 1 egg using Egg Replacer™ (by ENER-G, instructions on box)
Silken Tofu, amount equivalent to the amount of oil required by mix recipe
water, amount required by mix recipe

DIRECTIONS:

1. Preheat oven according to mix directions.

2. In a mini food processor or a blender combine silken tofu, Egg Replacer powder and water required for Egg Replacer, and ½ amount of water required for the mix. Blend to smooth consistency.

3. Combine mixture from step 2, remaining water for recipe, and brownie mix using a hand whisk. Mix until smooth.

4. Spray baking pan with non-stick spray or spread thin coat of tahini with fingers (actually works better).

5. Pour mixture into baking pan, smoothing out with spatula.

6. Bake for 3-5 minutes less than the amount required by mix.

Optional:

Crumble pieces of your favorite low-fat cookie on top of brownies before baking.

Rich Fudge Brownies from Scratch

INGREDIENTS:

1 cup silken tofu
equivalent of 4 eggs using Egg Replacer™ (by ENER-G, instructions on box)
2 cups sugar (or vanilla sugar)
2 tsp. real vanilla extract
¾ cup Dutch processed cocoa (Valrhona™ preferably)
1 cup all purpose, unbleached flour
½ tsp. baking powder
¼ tsp. salt
1 cup dark chocolate chips (Ghirardelli™ has great variety)

1/2 cup chopped walnuts (optional)

DIRECTIONS:

1. Preheat oven to 350°F.

2. In a mini food processor or a blender combine silken tofu and Egg Replacer powder and water required for Egg Replacer. Blend to smooth consistency.

3. In a bowl, combine mixture from step 2, sugar and vanilla. Blend using either a hand or a stand mixer.

4. In a separate bowl, sift all the dry ingredients together. Slowly and very gently mix into the wet ingredients from step two. Be sure all the ingredients are incorporated well without lumps, but do not over mix. Lastly blend in the cup of chocolate chips.

5. Pour mixture into a greased (use either cooking spray or tahini) 9x13 inch baking pan.

6. Bake for about 30 minutes or until toothpick comes out clean. Another way to tell with this recipe, since it is so rich, is that the middle will stop jiggling.

Carrot Cake with "Cream Cheese" Frosting

INGREDIENTS:

3 cups finely shredded organic carrots
2 cups all-purpose or cake flour
1 3/4 cups sugar
2 tsp, baking powder
1 tsp. baking soda
1/4 tsp. salt
1 1/2 tsp. ground cinnamon
juice of 1/2 orange
1/4 cup light olive oil
½ cup soft silken tofu
Equivalent of 3 eggs using Egg Replacer™ (by ENER-G, instructions on box)

½ cup chopped walnuts, optional
½ cup raisins, optional

"Cream Cheese" Frosting

8 ounces non-dairy cream cheese alternative, softened
5 cups confectioner's sugar, sifted
1 tsp. real vanilla extract

DIRECTIONS:

Cake

1. Preheat oven to 350 °F. Grease two 9 1/2 inch round baking pans.

2. In a mini food processor or a blender combine silken tofu, Egg Replacer powder and water required for Egg Replacer. Blend to smooth consistency.

3. Finely grate carrots and add juice of one-half orange. Carrots must be finely grated, otherwise they will sink to bottom of pan while baking.

4. Using a hand blender or Kitchen Aid (with batter blade), combine mixture from step 2 with sugar. Add carrots.

5. Sift together flour, baking powder, baking soda, salt, and cinnamon.

6. Blend dry ingredients into mixture from step 4. Add walnuts and raisins at this stage if desired.

7. Bake for 30-35 minutes or until toothpick comes out clean. Cool in pan for 10 minutes. Transfer to wire rack until cool.

Frosting:

1. Using electric mixer, slowly blend confectioner's sugar into cream cheese alternative. When all the sugar has been added, pour in vanilla extract.

2. Frost top of one cake and place second cake on top. Frost top and sides of the two layer cake. Cover with chopped walnuts if desired.

Chocolate Raspberry Sponge Cake

INGREDIENTS:

1 ¼ cups Dutch processed cocoa (Valrhona™, preferably)
1 ½ cups soy milk
1 cup boiling water
2/3 cup firm silken tofu
equivalent of 3 eggs using Egg Replacer™ (by ENER-G, instructions on box)
2 ½ cups vanilla, natural cane or white sugar
1 Tbs. real vanilla extract
2 ¼ cups all purpose flour
1 ½ tsp. baking powder
1 ½ tsp. baking soda
½ tsp. salt
8 ounces fresh raspberries
1/3 cup raspberry wine
1 ½ cup Newman-O's Tops and Bottoms™, ground
16 oz. Fat Free Cool Whip™
1/3 cup Dutch processed cocoa

DIRECTIONS:

1. Preheat oven to 350°F. Grease two 9 1/2 inch round baking pans.

2. In a large bowl, combine boiling water and cocoa. Using hand whisk, combine until all the cocoa is well incorporated. Add the soy milk and sugar.

3. In a mini food processor or a blender combine silken tofu, Egg Replacer powder, water required for Egg Replacer and vanilla extract. Blend to smooth consistency. Add to ingredients in step 2.

4. Sift together flour, baking powder, baking soda and salt Blend these dry ingredients into the wet ingredients. Pour into baking pans.

5. Bake for 35-40 minutes or until toothpick comes out clean. Cool in pan for 10 minutes. Transfer to wire rack until cool. Make sure cake is cold before proceeding to assembly (you can refrigerate for a few hours after cooling to room temperature.

Assembly:

1. In a food processor, grind enough Tops and Bottoms to make 1 ½ cups ground cookie crumbs.

2. Using an electric mixer, combine cool whip (properly defrosted) with cocoa until well combined. Cut each 9 inch cake in half to create 4 layers of sponge cake.

3. Lay down one layer of sponge cake. Brush generously with raspberry wine. Spread a layer of the chocolate frosting, add some fresh raspberries and sprinkle a generous handful of the cookie crumbs. Arrange two more layers like this. For the last, top layer, frost the entire cake, including sides. Place the raspberries on top of a layer of cookie crumbs.

Chocolate Sorbet

INGREDIENTS:

4 cups water
1 ¼ cups Dutch processed cocoa (Valrhona™ preferably)
2 cups vanilla or regular sugar
1 Tbs. instant espresso
2 Tbs. real vanilla extract
1/8 tsp. guar gum
1/8 tsp. xanthan gum
dash salt

DIRECTIONS:

1. Combine all ingredients, except gums into a pot. Heat to boiling and continue to cook until all contents are combined and dissolved. Turn off heat.

2. Using hand blender, add guar and xanthan gums and emulsify for approximately two minutes. Mixture will assume very thick, smooth consistency. Cool mixture for at least 4 hours or until near freezing.

3. Freeze mixture using highest quality ice cream machine you can, according to manufacturer's instructions.

Chocolate Tapioca Pudding

Servings: 4

INGREDIENTS:

4 cups soy milk
4 Tbs. Dutch processed cocoa (Valrhona™ preferably)
½ cup vanilla, natural cane or white sugar
6 Tbs. instant tapioca starch
2 tsp. instant espresso powder
1½ tsp. real vanilla extract
pinch salt

DIRECTIONS:

In a sauce pan, combine all ingredients, except vanilla and mix well with a whisk. Allow to sit for at least five minutes. Heat mixture to a boil, stirring constantly. Allow mixture to boil for one minute. Turn heat off, stir in vanilla and spoon pudding into serving dishes. Allow to set for 30 minutes. Enjoy warm or refrigerated.

HINT: For regular tapioca pudding, omit cocoa and espresso powder. Increase vanilla extract to 1 Tbs.

Grandma's Rice Pudding

Servings: 4

INGREDIENTS:

4 cups soy milk
½ cup medium or long grain rice
½ cup natural cane or white sugar
pinch sea salt
1-2 Tbs. orange blossom water
ground cinnamon

DIRECTIONS:

In a sauce pan, combine all ingredients, except orange blossom water and cinnamon.
Heat mixture to a boil, stirring constantly. Reduce to a simmer and cook until rice is very
tender and all the milk is absorbed. Stir in orange blossom water, using more or less,
according to your liking. Spoon pudding into serving dishes. Allow to set for at least
one hour. Sprinkle cinnamon on top of individual servings.

Marshmallows

Yield: 4 Dozen Marshmallows or about 1½ pounds

INGREDIENTS:

1 ½ cups vanilla sugar, unbleached or regular white
1 cup light corn syrup
3 Tbs. unflavored vegan gelatin (Emes Kosher Gelatin™: carageenan, locust bean gum, and malto-dextrin)
1 cup cold water
¼ tsp. sea salt
2 Tbs. real vanilla extract
½ cup cornstarch and ½ cup confectioner's sugar, sifted together

EQUIPMENT:

candy thermometer

DIRECTIONS:

1. In the bowl of a stand mixer, combine gelatin and ½ cup water. Mix well with the whisk attachment. Let stand for ½ hour.

2. Meanwhile combine the sugar, corn syrup, remaining ½ cup water and salt in a sauce pan. Stir over medium heat until the sugar is dissolved. When the mixture has begun to boil, cover for about 3 minutes. The steam will dissolve any sugar crystal remaining on the sides of the pan. Uncover and cook to the firmball stage, 244°F, using the candy thermometer.

3. As soon as the mixture reaches the firmball stage, remove from heat. Slowly add the syrup to the gelatin mixture while beating at high speed. Continue to beat at high speed for about 15 minutes after all the syrup has been added. The mixture should be fluffy white and will have tripled in size. If you stop beating before this point you get marshmallow fluff (makes for tasty "fluffer nutter" sandwiches). If you overbeat, you will have very chewy marshmallows. Gently incorporate the vanilla extract when you are done beating.

4. Dust a sheet pan with the cornstarch/confectioner's sugar mixture. With a spatula spread out the marshmallow batter. Shake the pan to evenly distribute the batter. Dust the top with more of the corn starch mixture. Allow to sit overnight at room temperature to set. Lay out onto a board the next morning, and cut into squares using a metal wire or warm knife.

HINTS:

1. I find that the marshmallows are perfectly edible within one hour of finishing the recipe. However, they will be slightly firmer if allowed to set overnight.

2. I found that using a wire to cut the marshmallows works much better than a knife. Dust the cut marshmallows with more of the corn starch mixture to prevent them from sticking.

3. You can add any flavoring you like instead of vanilla extract. I like to make Peppermint Marshmallows, using peppermint oil (about 10 drops for this recipe), and put them in my hot cocoa.

4. The only source of Emes Kosher Gelatin I know of is the Internet. You may want to try your local health foods store. If you really can not get your hands on some, this recipe works just fine with regular gelatin made from animal products.

Old Fashioned Popcorn/Kettle Corn

Servings: 2

INGREDIENTS:

1/3 cup of popcorn kernels
1 tsp. extra-virgin or light olive oil
¼ tsp. fine popcorn salt (Diamond™ table salt)
2 packets Splenda™ brand sweetener (equivalent of 4 tsp. sugar)

DIRECTIONS:

1. In the heaviest pot you have that is at least 3 qt. size, add all the ingredients. Turn burner to medium and cover the pot. Do not leave the stovetop. Popcorn will cook in a just a few minutes. Continuously shake the pot over the heat until all the popcorn stops popping. If you want just regular popcorn, leave out the sweetener. Do not use sugar as it will burn over the stovetop. Kettle corn made in a real kettle is usually made over very high heat and cooked in a well ventilated room.

2. Ingredients I like on my popcorn: cayenne pepper, oregano, nutritional yeast.

Peppermint Hot Chocolate

Servings: 4

INGREDIENTS:

4 cups soy milk
4 Tbs. Dutch processed cocoa (Valrhona™ preferably)
4 Tbs. vanilla sugar, unbleached or white
2 tsp. real vanilla extract
pinch salt
Peppermint Marshmallows (see below)

DIRECTIONS:

In a sauce pan, combine all ingredients, except vanilla and mix well with a whisk. Heat mixture to completely dissolve sugar and incorporate the cocoa. Do not boil the mixture. Serve in individual mugs.

In order to make Peppermint Marshmallows follow the recipe for Marshmallows and use about 10 drops of peppermint oil instead of vanilla extract (peppermint oil is highly concentrated. It can be found at most specialty food stores). Cut the marshmallows into ½ inch cubes and add a handful to each cup. If you do not want to make the marshmallows, you can simply add a drop or two of peppermint oil to each cup of hot chocolate.

"Rice Krispies" Treats

Servings: 8-12

INGREDIENTS:

6 cups Kellogg's Rice Krispies™ cereal
2 Tbs. vegetable margarine
10 ounces or 4 cups or 1/3 recipe Marshmallows (vegan)

DIRECTIONS:

In a large sauce pan, combine margarine and marshmallows. Cook over low heat until marshmallows are completely dissolved. Turn heat off and stir in the cereal. When adequately combined, spread mixture onto a sheet pan lined with wax or parchment paper. Use another sheet of wax or parchment paper on top of the treats to spread into a uniform mold, about 2 inches thick. Allow to set and cool for about 20 minutes. Then cut into individual servings.

Whole Wheat Pie Crust

Makes top and bottom crust for one pie.

INGREDIENTS:

2 cups whole wheat pastry flour
1 cup almonds
3 ounces soy milk
2 Tbs. real maple syrup
¼ tsp. sea salt
½ tsp. baking powder

DIRECTIONS:

In a food processor, grind the almonds with the salt into a paste, with as smooth a consistency as possible. In separate bowl, sift together the flour and baking powder. To the almond paste in the food processor, slowly add the flour. Process until all the almond paste is blended into the flour. Do not over-process, otherwise the crust will be chewy. The flour at this point should be mealy and flaky. In a separate bowl, whisk together soy milk and maple syrup. Slowly blend these into the flour/almond mixture. Very slowly process until the mixture just forms a ball (you may need to add an extra tablespoon of soy milk). Again, you do not want to overwork the dough. Wrap the dough in plastic wrap and refrigerate for at least one hour. Dough also freezes well if you want to make it ahead of time.

For More Information…

Get more information, the latest heart news, heart disease treatments, and more heart-smart recipes and healthy living advice on the Internet at:

www.DiagnosisHeart.com

It's Free!

You'll find the latest news on advanced cardiac surgery, dietary breakthroughs, discussion forums where you can ask your questions and have both peer and expert responses and much more.

Want to Be In-the-Know?
Sign up for our free newsletter to be kept up to date on our latest projects, cardiac nutrition and much more!

Sign up at http://www.DiagnosisHeart.com

Notes

Notes

Notes